BLUEBERRIES AND BEARS AND MY BROTHER'S SHOES

By

Susan L. Pare'

Blueberries and Bears and My Brother's Shoes

Blueberries and Bears and My Brother's Shoes

MORE BOOKS BY THIS AUTHOR

Red, White, and Blue
(A Short Story)

She Never Stopped Talking

Red

The House on Ludington Street

What's Behind the Screen Door?

The Mayor's Son

Willerton Woods

Cowtown

Floating Face Down
A Sheriff "Cowboy" Berkson Mystery Novel – Book Three

Let's Play Autopsy

A Bad Week In Hollister
A Sheriff "Cowboy" Berkson Mystery Novel – Book Two

Don't Smother Your Mother
A Sheriff "Cowboy" Berkson Mystery Novel – Book One

Crossing Sydney

Blueberries and Bears and My Brother's Shoes

TABLE OF CONTENTS

I've taken a step back from writing another mystery novel to bring you this mostly true story about growing up in the '50s. I hope you find the departure from the norm enjoyable. I'll be back soon with another mystery novel, so keep an eye out. But, for now, I'm proud to present:

Blueberries and Bears

And

My Brother's Shoes

By

Susan L. Pare'

Blueberries and Bears and My Brother's Shoes

For My Sons

Bruce

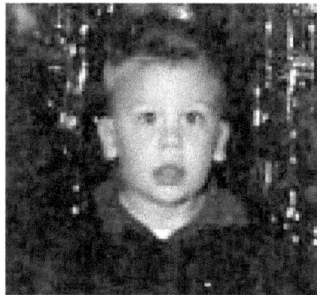

Jon

Perry

Blueberries and Bears and My Brother's Shoes

The Second Time Around

When I originally wrote this book in 2015, it was for my sons, their families, and a few close friends. I wanted to share with them what it was like growing up in the Pare house in the '40s and '50s.

When my dad died, I realized that I knew very little about what his life had been like before I was born. When my mom died, I think I knew everything about her, as she never stopped talking. However, I am not sure how much she told me is actually true.

I realized after I finished writing this book years ago, that I had probably had months of therapy without even seeing a psychiatrist. The first edition had twice as many chapters as this edition. That is because I have thrown away all the garbage that took place in my life. After getting it out of my system and writing it down, I found out that the garbage was no longer important. To me, writing this was definitely a healing process. I think you probably know what I mean. Most of us have been there.

I realized, once I tossed out those worthless, non-productive chapters, that perhaps my life was probably much different from the lives of many of the kids with whom I grew up.

Therefore, here is the rewrite of my first book. It is mostly about growing up, but I have added a few chapters that have nothing to do with my life or me. I'm not a very good poet, but I enjoy writing them. Feel free to skip them if you want. You won't hurt my feelings. Not everyone likes poetry and mine are a little out of the norm. However, you might enjoy one or two of them.

I come from a family of seven. Of the five Pare children that mistakenly entered this world (according to my mother), I am exactly in the middle. I've heard that being a middle child is hard for some, but that wasn't necessarily the case for me. Although none of us was spoiled, I was my father's favorite, and my siblings were well aware of that fact.

These little chapters are mostly about those siblings and me growing up. Some of them are dead now. It's all part of the process and God's plan. After all, you can't have life without death being your final chapter.

A lot of the people who walked through my life are gone now. There are also those who I've killed off in my mind. It makes life so much easier.

I believe that chapters in a book can be like time periods of your life. They can be short or long, funny or sad, clear or fuzzy.

So, to begin. I don't remember being born but I sure recollect the bullshit story I was told

Awakening

I'm not asleep, yet I'm not awake. I'm in that place where I haven't decided if I should open my eyes and meet the day or continue to lie in bed and let my mind wander to unknown places. This is the time of day that my mind starts to race. This is the time when old friends show up and we do what we did all over again. And, sometimes I see dead people.

It is while I am in this state of in-between that my mind drifts back to memories that should have been long forgotten. Sometimes a memory is something you remember being told but don't actually remember yourself. So, I guess you are having a recollection of being told something but not the actual memory. I think, though, that if you can see that memory in your head, like a snapshot, then you must be remembering.

Pare or Pare'

My father, born Arthur Joseph Pare in 1906, was running a gas station in Peshtigo, Wisconsin when he met my mother. Her name was Ruth Clara Anna Geyer, born in 1914. I never heard the true story of how my parents met. Dad was eight years older than my mother and she married him when she was only nineteen years old. Neither of her parents, the Reverend Kurt Geyer nor his wife, Elsie Kionka Geyer, were happy with her choice. As the years passed, they accepted him, but barely.

Picture – Dad's Texaco Station in Peshtigo

My father was a Catholic. My mother was the daughter of a Lutheran minister. Dad's church never recognized the marriage and dad did not go to church for the eighteen years that they were married. Once they divorced, he started going to church again.

4

Picture – My father Arthur Pare' – Around 64 or 65 years old.

Picture – My mother Ruth Clara Anna Geyer Pare' Roedle Nitzchke – Around 65 years old.

The name Pare' is French. Dad's ancestors migrated to Canada from France. There has always been a debate on how to pronounce the name Pare'. The French pronunciation sounds like Par-ray. We simply said Pare, which we pronounced Perry. If someone called us Pear, they were usually strangers. The true spelling should have the diacritic above the e.

Of the five Pare children that survived their upbringing, Kurt Arthur was the first to arrive in 1934. My parents lived in Peshtigo, Wisconsin at the time. He was named Kurt after my grandfather, Rev. Kurt Geyer, and Arthur after my dad.

I believe Virginia Elsie, who came along a few years later in 1936, was also born while my parents lived in Peshtigo. Her middle name Elsie was my grandmother's first name.

I, Susan Lee, was born in Bonners Ferry, Idaho in 1939. I was named Susan after my dad's stepmother, Suzie Albrecht.

Carol Ann was born in 1942. We were living in Rhinelander, Wisconsin at the time. She was not named after anyone important like the rest of us.

George Emmet was born in 1944 in Kalispell, Montana. We were living in Somers, Montana. George was named after dad's stepfather, George Albrecht.

I am the middle child. There are five years between Kurt and me and five years between George and me.

From 1939 to 1949, we moved seven times. We lived in Idaho, Colorado, Wisconsin, Montana, Michigan, Montana, and Wisconsin.

BONNERS FERRY, IDAHO

Picture - Ruth and Susan

1939

The river was swift and angry, as it was every year when the winter snow thawed and the spring rains added their raindrops to its rushing waters. These same waters swept under the bridge that divided the town of Bonners Ferry, Idaho, and sometimes, they heartlessly took the lives of careless adults and children. Every year, the river claimed one or two residents of the town, usually children playing too close to the shoreline. Indians, living upstream on the Kootenai Indian Reservation, would also occasionally lose one of their own, while trying to escape the unforgiving waters of this river.

This April, the river was extremely high, flooding everything along its banks. The gravel road the man drove on was now mostly mud and he was overly cautious, as the slightest mishap could be his last. He had experienced many narrow escapes, due to deer running across the road in front of his pickup truck and this certainly was no time for an accident.

He glanced over at the river and wondered how much higher it could possibly get before it crested. Then, he noticed a small raft with a bundle strapped on it, floating in the river. He pulled over to the side of the road and got out of his truck, hoping to get a better view. At that particular moment, the raft washed up against the shore and became stuck in the mud.

As he walked closer to the river, the man thought he heard a slight sound over the rushing waters. He gazed down at the bundle strapped to the raft and his heart started to pound as he saw movement. He made it down the slippery bank to the raft, took his jackknife out

8

of his pocket, and cut the strap covering the bundle. He grabbed the bundle and managed to get back up the muddy, slippery hill without falling.

He put the small bundle on the ground next to his car and unwrapped it. Lying there, soaking wet from the dirty river water, was a little baby girl. Her dark hair and brown skin left no doubt that she was from the reservation.

He opened the car door and laid the crying baby on the seat beside him. As he glanced at her, the baby suddenly stopped her crying and smiled. "I'm going to call you Susan, after my stepmother," the man said softly and drove on towards home.

The Introduction Explains It All

The introduction you read is the actual story my mother told me when I was a little girl. Yes. I believed it. I was only a couple of years old.

Little did I know that this story, plus the dozens of others I heard growing up, would mold me into the slightly non-conformist person that I am today. It took a while, but I finally learned that I manage life's trials and tribulations so much better when I move away from reality and join the lighter, happier side of my brain.

Picture – Virginia, Kurt, Susan

I always try to separate myself from those who wish me harm. It works for me and being able to see the humor in most things has, most likely, saved me from being institutionalized.

"Laugh and the world laughs with you. Weep, and you weep alone." (Ella Wheeler Wilcox; November 5, 1850 – October 30, 1919)

Never were words more honestly written than those by Ms. Wilcox. No one wants to be around a woman who is babbling like a child. But everyone wants to be there when the clown starts the show.

After all, what is funnier than seeing a person slip on the ice and fall down? Or, watching eight pallbearers drop a casket and see a body roll out onto the ground? You clearly gotta laugh.

RHINELANDER, WISCONSIN

Picture – Susan – Three years old

A Dime a Dance – My First Real Memory

I was considered small for my age. And, I was skinny. Sometimes my dad called me 'Runt'. I didn't like it, but it was better than some of his other nicknames for me, like Susan McGooson. I was also very smart. At only four years old, I knew how to read, add and subtract, and I was learning my multiplication tables. By the time I entered kindergarten, I knew the tables through ten.

Now, understand that this wasn't due to the fact that my mother spent a lot of time with me teaching me all these things. It was because I had an older brother and sister who liked to play 'school'. I was always a student and what they learned in school, I learned at home. Or, else.

And, also, at a very young age, I had learned what the inside of a tavern looked like.

Taverns were different back in the 1940s. Times were tough and most parents couldn't afford babysitters when they went out. My parents were no exception. When my parents went out in the evening, it was usually to a tavern to drink beer or a few highballs and they dragged us three kids with them. We would sit at a table if one was available, but most of the time my parents sat at the bar and us three kids sat on the floor.

My Uncle Roland, who was my mother's brother, had given me a little grass skirt. I would put it on and pretend to dance the hula around the house. One night, my mother put my grass skirt in her purse and brought it with us when we went out to the tavern.

After the bar had filled up with the regular drinkers, my mother put that grass skirt on me, pushed me out onto the dance floor, and told me to dance. I've been told I danced my silly little version of the hula and people threw their change at me. Pennies, nickels, and an occasional dime. It wasn't a lot of money by today's standards but it was enough to keep my parents drinking for the rest of the night.

So, we have my brother and sister sitting on the dirty floor of a tavern while I danced my little ass off for beer money for my parents. Isn't that a precious picture?

It's true. Even now, when I close my eyes, I can see the inside of that tavern. It's like a snapshot. I can't see the whole tavern. I see a table with two chairs sitting near the dance floor. I see the jukebox and my parents dancing the polka.

I don't know if this is a good memory or a bad one. It is, however, my first memory.

Take Her Back

When I was three years and eight months old, I spent two wonderful weeks with my grandparents. Grandma and grandpa looked exactly like grandparents are supposed to look. Grandma's big bosoms were like pillows on which to rest my head, and grandpa's sizable lap was great to sit on while being entertained. One game he played with me, while I was lap-sitting, was to have me look away while he took his teeth out. Then, I would look back, see him with no teeth, and squeal. I would look away again and, when I looked back, his teeth would be back in his mouth. Such magic! Such fun!

I spent those two weeks being spoiled. Being spoiled for two weeks probably wouldn't have been a big deal if I hadn't already been spoiled rotten. For almost four years, I had been the baby of the family and I had received a lot of attention. Now, I was getting all of the attention from grandma and grandpa. So, when they told me they were going to take me back home to Rhinelander, I absolutely refused. After they told me there was a big surprise waiting for me, I couldn't wait to get in that car to leave. I pestered them the whole ride back home to tell me what the surprise was but they never gave in.

As soon as we walked through the front door, my parents took my grandparents into a small room where there was a crib. Everyone was oohing and aahing and saying how cute something was. My dad finally reached down, picked me up, and said, "Hey, Runt, this is your new baby sister that's come to live with us."

"Take her back," I demanded.

Carol had arrived.

I was tall enough so I could reach through the slats of her crib and touch her. I found great joy in pinching her whenever I thought no one was looking. She would cry and then I would pretend I was rubbing her little back to make her feel better. I was never caught.

It took a long time for me to adjust to the fact that she was staying. They were not giving her back and I was no longer the center of attention. I was angry with my parents for a long time and spent a lot of time pouting. I ran away for a little while, too, and hid under the neighbor's porch for what seemed like hours but it was probably only a few minutes.

There have been times when I wonder why I didn't forego the pinching and simply smother her in her crib right then and there. However, that's a different story for another time.

SOMERS, MONTANA – FLATHEAD LAKE

Picture – Carol – One and a half years old.

Karma Can Be Painful

My fourth and last sibling, George, arrived into our family while were living in a house on Flathead Lake, in 1944. The home dad rented was about three miles outside of Somers, Montana. I barely remember George joining our family so it obviously was not as traumatic to me as when Carol was born.

I have to admit that Carol was cute, a little pudgy, and had big eyes. I mean really big eyes. When we were a little older, I would tell her that she had cow's eyes. This would set her off and she'd have one of her dramatic hissy fits.

From the time she could put a sentence together, she would say she wanted to be a blond and a movie star when she grew up. She managed to accomplish the blond part, thanks to hair color. However, even though she acted her way through a great deal of her life (at least in my eyes) she was never a movie star.

Back to 1944. The house we were living in had floor registers and, as with most old houses, the furnace was in the basement. In the winter, when that furnace was roaring those floor registers got hot – really, really hot – and we knew to stay away from them or we could get burned.

And, of course, that is exactly what happened when Carol fell on the floor register in the living room and landed on her butt-naked little ass. I don't know why she didn't have panties on but she didn't. She screamed and mother ran into the room demanding to know what happened.

"Susa," the little liar sobbed and pointed at me.

It was a bad burn. Bad enough that she had to see a doctor and it left a checkerboard scar on her ass, which was visible for years. It could still be there for all I know. It's a miracle that I don't have a permanent scar of my mother's handprint on my ass.

No one ever believed that I didn't do it.

HOUGHTON, MICHIGAN,

Picture – Kurt, Carol, Susan

Five Years After the Flood

Shortly after George was born and Carol's ass healed, we moved again. This time we wound up in Houghton, Michigan, where I started school. I was smart even before I had to be. I knew arithmetic and was reading at a third-grade level by the time I entered kindergarten. At one point, they considered advancing me a grade or two but my mother absolutely forbade it.

Having an older brother and sister was probably one of the reasons I was so advanced. One of the games we played at home was school. Kurt and Virginia would switch being the teacher but I was always a student. Obviously, I was learning what they had already learned.

Shortly after I started kindergarten, my teacher asked every child to stand up, one at a time, and tell their classmates about their families. I could hardly wait for my turn and, when the teacher called on me, I stood up and proudly blurted out, "My name is Susan. I have two brothers and two sisters. I was born on the Kootenai Indian Reservation in Idaho and I am an Indian. My dad found me floating down the river on a raft during a flood and saved me. My dad runs a logging camp and my mother likes to have coffee with the neighbors."

I guess my teacher talked to my mother after that discourse because that night my parents sat me down and explained to me that they had been teasing me. For all these frickin' years I had been lied to. I was not a full-blooded Indian, I was not found floating down a river on a raft and I was their natural child.

"Shit," I responded. My mother informed me that

if I ever said that word again, she would wash my mouth out with soap. Of course, I said shit again and even though my father thought it was funny, my mother still washed out my mouth with soap.

I have to say that I enjoyed my years as a 'full-blooded Indian'. I looked the part with hair that was straight and so dark it was almost black. I was tanned so dark by the summer sun that I was brown all year long. When we played cowboys and Indians, I was always Tonto.

I had a rude awakening that day. Parents lie. To their kids. Why was it okay for my parents to lie to me but if I lied to them, I got in trouble? Although I didn't know it at the time, I had clearly found out what 'double standard' meant.

Note: I am aware that the correct terminology as of this minute is American-Indian. Back in the early 1940s, we said Indian. I do not know what it might be when you read this book. Please do not write or email me with comments.

Let the Show Begin

It was 1944 and my older brother and sister and I, along with three or four of our neighborhood friends, were putting on a neighborhood musical. The words and melodies of the songs had been memorized and we had practiced our parts for days. 'The Daring Young Man on the Flying Trapeze', 'A Bicycle Built for Two', and 'Let me Call You Sweetheart' were a few of the songs that we would be performing that afternoon.

With dad's permission, we had confiscated the garage and turned it into a theatre. The stage was at the farthest end of the garage and an old blanket had been hung as a stage curtain. The rest of the garage was where our audience would sit on chairs we had begged and borrowed from our families.

My brother, Kurt, who was ten at the time, could not sing worth a damn so he was in charge of the production. He made signs advertising the show and posted them around the neighborhood. In addition, because he was the oldest, he put himself in charge of collecting the admission money from our paying customers.

Someone had decided that the entry fee would be two cents for kids and a nickel for adults. We weren't sure if anyone would come if they had to pay but the whole point of the show was to make money. We had practiced our asses off and we were ready to entertain. The performance was being held on a Saturday afternoon in hopes that we would have a crowd.

The big day arrived. I was so excited I could barely eat my lunch. The minute we were excused from the table we ran to the garage to get ready, even though the show didn't begin for another two hours. Our costumes were old clothes ready for the trash. Many safety pins had been used so the dresses would fit our little bodies and so we wouldn't trip over the long hems. Some of us wore fancy old hats donated by our mothers. We spent a lot of time putting on lipstick and rouge and we probably looked like clowns but we thought we looked like movie stars.

A half-hour before show time, our first customers arrived – and they just kept coming. We filled the garage that day with mothers, fathers, and kids. They were old, young, and in-between and there were smokers and non-smokers. We were going to be stars.

We were ready to perform but scared to death as we stood behind the blanket that served as our curtain. Right before the show started, I stuck my face partway through a hole in the blanket to look at the crowd. And, some son of a bitch who was smoking touched my nose with the lit end of his cigarette.

I let out a scream and fell backward into a girl on the stage. As she attempted to steady herself, she grabbed the blanket/curtain, pulled it down, and fell headfirst onto a woman sitting in the first row. Madder than hell and ready to kill, I pulled up my skirt and went for the boy who had burned me with the cigarette. He took off, knocking my brother over as he ran out of the garage. My brother landed on his ass, dropping his little tin can holding the money, and pennies and nickels went flying all over the driveway. He started to cry. My sister, Virginia, decided the show must go on and started to sing. I kept on running after the kid who had burned me with no idea what I would do if I caught him.

Dad finally stepped in and yelled, "Show's over, folks. Time to go home."

The audience started screaming at my brother, who was on his hands and knees trying to pick up the dropped money. They wanted their money back.

My idiot sister just stayed on the stage and kept on singing.

I never caught that kid, which was probably lucky for me. I was, however, blamed for the whole fiasco. It seems that peeking through that hole in the blanket and being burned on my nose was my fault.

It was days like this that I wished I was back on the reservation with my real family.

Grandpa's Church

Even when my grandparents were young, they seemed old to me. They were strict, being old-school Germans and after the age of about nine or ten, my grandfather scared me. Grandpa was a Lutheran minister for over fifty years. He spent forty-eight of those years preaching in the same church in Peshtigo, Wisconsin.

Picture -My grandparents, Rev. and Mrs. Kurt Geyer. Grandpa celebrating 50 years as a minister.

Grandpa's office was in his house. It was understood, when we were visiting on weekends, that we kids must stay clear of the house on Saturdays while Grandpa wrote his Sunday sermons. So, just like at home, we would run wild for hours at a time.

It was wonderful when there was going to be a wedding or funeral and the Fellowship Hall had been set up for some type of reception. We would sneak in the back door and start sampling the goods. We were usually kicked out after we started to get on everyone's nerves but not before we had satisfied our cravings for sweets. Germans and sweets are a marriage made in heaven.

We always went to church on Sunday. Mother would march us into church and sit our asses down in a pew, usually on the pulpit side where Grandpa had an unobstructed view of us. We never talked out loud, we barely moved a muscle, and we listened hard. We knew he was watching and we had learned the hard way to behave in church. After the services were over and we sat down for dinner (now known as lunch), Grandpa was going to ask questions. And, we better know the answers.

Picture – Kurt, Grandma Geyer, Virginia, Carol, Susan

Grandma was the church organist and she directed the choir. She was very talented, as was my grandfather who had a beautiful singing voice. To this day, I cannot hear the song, 'How Great Thou Art,' without crying. He sang this song the last time I saw him before he died.

Dad never came to church with us. He was a Catholic and he mostly went downtown and had a few beers on Sunday mornings, while we got religion.

Picture -Houghton, Michigan – Mother, Dad, Kurt, Gini, Carol, and Susan

Wild and Free

I started school in Houghton, Michigan, in 1944. The country was in the middle of a war, there was rationing, food stamps, and times were tough for most families. I know we must have struggled to get by as I got my older brother's and sister's hand-me-downs to wear, which included my brother's old shoes. I started school wearing my brother's old shoes and no one made fun of me. As I said, times were tough.

When WWII ended in 1945, we all ran around in front of our house waving little flags and yelling, "The war is over."

However, it is the summers there that I remember the most. We played outside a lot with the neighbor kids and playing cowboys and Indians was always my favorite. Sometimes, we would be gone all day. My older brother, sister, and I would get up early. We would make sandwiches of bread and oleo and, occasionally, we had some homemade jelly. The best – the very very best was on the rare occasions when we had sugar in the house. Mother would sprinkle a little sugar on our bread and it tasted like heaven.

We explored the woods behind our house, climbed rocky cliffs, ran in the fields, and played in our own special stream that we had found hidden in a meadow. We were sure we were the only ones that had ever been there. We followed the smell of spearmint that grew close to the stream and, when we found some, we chewed on the leaves.

I can't remember any of us getting hurt while we went on our adventures. Maybe an occasional fall from the rocky cliff gave us a scrape or two, but never anything serious. We ran wild, totally unsupervised until it got dark outside. No boogieman got us. No wild animals attacked us. No adults were allowed.

Our playground was huge and it belonged to us.

Well, Hello Dolly

The weekend my Aunt Meg got married, it was complete chaos at my grandparents' house. My mother was in the wedding party and had no time for us kids. Dad was probably downtown having a few beers. Whatever the case, we were totally underfoot and in everyone's way.

My Uncle Roland stepped up to the plate and volunteered to get us three older kids out of everyone's hair. Off we went to town to get an ice cream cone. Suddenly, in a spirit of unprecedented generosity, my uncle told us that we could pick out any toy we wanted. I guess, since we were in the Five and Dime Store, he was pretty sure that none of the toys would cost very much

This was a great treat. It wasn't even Christmas or my birthday and I was going to get a present.

I had never been a girly girl. I didn't like playing with dolls. I'd rather play hit your brother than play house. But, when I saw my 'gift', I fell in love. I had never seen a doll like this before. My uncle did a lot of talking trying to convince me to pick out something else. No way! He said we could have whatever we wanted and I wanted what I saw. No amount of arguing could change my mind.

The war had ended and I had celebrated by waving a flag in our front yard in Houghton. I had heard talk among the adults about our soldiers coming home. For the first time in my life, I wanted a doll. This doll, however, wasn't a baby doll or even a girl doll. It was a boy doll. He was about 12 inches tall, he was dressed like a soldier, and he was black.

I only had that doll for a couple of days. He disappeared shortly after we left Peshtigo and went back home.

My Brother's Shoes

When I was little, I didn't know what poor was. I can't recall kids making fun of me because of the clothes I wore. Sometimes my dresses were hand-me-downs from my older sister and sometimes mother made them from flour sacks. I can't remember that it ever bothered me that I had to wear shoes my brother had outgrown. I was more concerned about not getting into trouble than what kind of clothes I wore. At least, until the day I went to a birthday party.

Picture – I'm sitting on the front porch of our house in Houghton, MI. Probably five years old.

Gretchen was my best friend in Houghton. We went to school together and played together. She lived a little way down the hill from me in a big house that always looked so pretty from the outside. We never played inside our houses. Winter, spring, summer, or fall, our playground was always outside.

Gretchen was turning seven and I had been invited to her birthday party.

Holy shit! When I walked inside her house, I couldn't believe it. I was six years old, but I immediately knew that this was a different world from mine. It was the most beautiful house I had ever seen.

That afternoon, we played pin the tail on the donkey. Gretchen's mother made sure that everyone won at least once and got a prize. We sat at a beautiful table and had ice cream and cake. There were place settings and at each setting was another little gift for the guest. I walked out of that party with more presents than I had ever received at Christmas.

In my six-year-old head, I thought everyone lived like my family. I had been subjected to a world totally different from mine. I had sat on beautiful chairs and walked on soft carpets. I ate cake and ice cream and we didn't even have sugar in our house.

When the party was over, I walked back up the hill towards my house, with its bare, cold floors, and I realized that we were poor. For the first time ever, I was ashamed of my shoes.

KALISPELL, MONTANA

Picture – Our house in Kalispell, MT - - 1948

Two at a Time

When I was in the third grade, dad quit running logging camps and started a new job working as a lumber salesman. This change took us back out west to Kalispell, Montana. We lived there while I was in the third and fourth grades. This new job also meant that he was away from home a lot more.

We weren't far from Glacier National Park and I spent many days there. I'd sit on the ground and watch dad fish. Watching him cast that fishing line into streams and creeks was like watching a moving piece of art. He could land it exactly in the right spot and rainbow and brown trout were frequently the catch of the day. Dad could have starred in the movie, 'A River Runs Through It'. He was that good, if not better.

Western Montana was beautiful with forests, mountains, glacier-filled lakes, and fast-moving streams and rivers. Back in the forties, when we traveled the back roads and got thirsty, dad would stop the car near a creek or a stream. We'd go running to the water and cup our hands and drink that icy, cold water. As we drank our fill, it wasn't unusual to see a rainbow trout go swimming by.

There were trips with only Dad, Kurt, and me and trips with Dad, Virginia, and me. But, sometimes, I was Dad's only traveling companion. We stopped at sawmills along the way as Dad did his business. I loved it. I was eight or nine years old and, as we drove the back roads of Montana, he taught me how to identify every tree in the woods. Not simply a pine tree, mind you, but what kind of a pine tree.

I almost learned the hard way not to walk behind a horse. I was missed by inches by a kicking horse when I walked behind it. Dad managed to pull me out of the way just in time.

He talked and I listened and learned. He could be fun to be with and sometimes he bought me Cracker Jacks. Cracker Jack prizes were great back then.

Picture -Dad with Virginia and Susan

Sometimes, after we had crossed a little wooden bridge with a stream running under it, dad would stop the car. He'd open the trunk, take out a fishing pole, and start fishing. Usually, he would string a line on a stick that he cut from a tree and make me a fishing pole. I would sit on the bridge and fish. I never baited my hook, though. He always had to do it for me.

There was one occasion when dad and I went fishing on Swan Lake. We were sitting in a rowboat, in the middle of this beautiful lake, fishing and it was lunchtime. Dad handed me his pole to hold while he was opening a can of beans. I got a strike on both poles at the same time and we brought in two nice rainbow trout. Of course, dad had to take them off the hooks. I wouldn't do that either.

Life was good when I was young and it was only the two of us.

Drunk as a Skunk

From the time I can remember, my father always gave me a sip of his beer. When I got a little older, dad would pour a couple of swallows into a little glass and give that to me to drink. He was either trying to make me feel grown up or was paving the way for me to become an alcoholic.

The first time I got drunk, I was in the fourth grade. My father did it to me. I'm not sure if it was on purpose, an accident, or meant to be funny.

We were living in Kalispell and it was a holiday. We had company for dinner and the adults and older kids were eating in the dining room. I was sitting at the little table in the kitchen along with my younger brother and sister.

After I saw my dad pour some purple liquid into wine glasses, I asked him if I could have some. He graciously poured a jelly glass full of red wine and I drank every drop like it was water.

We had peas for dinner that day and I couldn't get the peas to stay on my fork. I thought this was extremely funny until I fell off my stool and landed hard on the kitchen floor. My head was spinning and staying on the stool was no longer an option. I couldn't. It seems I was the entertainment for the day, as the people sitting at the adult table thought it was extremely funny. My feelings were hurt and I couldn't stand up, so I stayed on the floor and cried.

When my mother finally decided to help me, I threw up all over her. Then, of course, my mother yelled at my father for giving me the wine and a big fight started.

Picture - Sixty-eight years after we lived there. The house is the same. There is still an alley behind the house, but the garage is gone. So is the church that was across the street

Peddling Our Asses

I ran away from home twice between the ages of three and eight. The first time was when Carol was deposited into my life. I ran away and hid under the neighbor's porch. I was only gone for a few minutes so it probably doesn't really count as 'running away'. I was more pissed off than anything and wanted some attention.

The second time I ran away I was eight years old. Virginia was eleven. I have no idea what had transpired this time to make Virginia and I hate our mother enough to run away but we were in a definite hate mother phase. Perhaps, it was only Virginia doing the hating and I went along for the ride. Whatever - we decided we were going to run away and stay away and live with people who liked us. Forever.

This escape was planned to the last detail. Dad was out of town. Virginia had a bike but I didn't, so we borrowed one from a friend and hid it in our garage. The garage was off an alley that ran behind our house so there was no reason for mother to go in there and find the borrowed bike.

Our house in Kalispell was located directly across the street from our church. Mother was singing in the choir that Sunday, so Kurt was sitting in a pew watching Carol and George. Virginia and I were upstairs in the balcony of the church. Virginia was writing mother a note telling her how much we hated her and that we were running away forever and that she shouldn't try to find us. We snuck out of church early, went home, and put the note on the table for her to find.

Then we got the bikes out of the garage and we headed out.

Picture -Virginia and Susan - Kalispell

We biked about fourteen miles that day. It was hot out and we stopped once at a tavern and went in and bought some pop. No one questioned an eight and an eleven-year-old stopping in for a drink. Different times, for sure.

We arrived at Oursland's home exhausted and hungry. Naturally, we took them by surprise but they welcomed us like this was an everyday occurrence.

Mrs. Oursland was boiling eggs when we got there and she totally forgot about them until the stink of rotten eggs took over the house.

Mrs. Oursland fixed us something to eat and then Virginia told them we were going to stay and live with them. They told us we were going home.

When Mr. and Mrs. Oursland dropped us and the bikes off at home, my mother hugged us and told us how worried she was and how much we had scared her. She told the Ourslands how sorry she was for the trouble we put them through and she thanked them over and over for taking such good care of us. As soon as Mr. and Mrs. Oursland left, my mother started screaming about how she had made plans for that Sunday afternoon and how we had ruined her day.

My mother gave it to Virginia pretty bad that day. I wasn't even slapped.

My mother was always frustrated over something and she took her frustrations out on us kids, but Virginia seemed to be her main target. And, even though mother treated her like shit throughout her entire life, Virginia was always there for her when she needed something. Until the day mother died, at the age of 98 years and 362 days, Virginia kept coming back for more.

Virginia died two months after my mother. I guess she needed to be with her mother, once again.

Big Red Bows

We were still living in Kalispell when mother disappeared for the third time. This time when she left George was three, Carol was five, I was eight, Virginia was eleven and Kurt was thirteen.

We rarely went anywhere without my mother, so it seemed strange when my dad took all of us kids out on a Sunday afternoon for a ride. When we finally got back to the house and walked in, my mother was on the bathroom floor trying to wipe up all the blood. She said that she had broken a mirror and cut her leg. She had a horrible cut and dad took her to the doctor for stitches.

After her leg was better, she left my dad for the third time. I don't know if it was a surprise to my father. I have to think it was but sometimes I think she was planning to leave the day dad took us for that ride.

It was in the fall and she was still gone doing her 'recovering from her kids' thing at Christmas time. She was in Colorado this time and we were excited when a package with Christmas gifts arrived from her. Virginia, Carol, and I received white long-sleeved blouses with big red bows that tied at the neck. She had made them for us and we were excited that we had new blouses to wear to church on Christmas Eve.

We were supposed to go to church that Christmas Eve. Kurt, Virginia, and I had parts to perform in the service. Even though the church was directly across the street from our house, dad had told us we could not leave the house until he got home. When he finally walked through the door and stumbled into bed, the church service was over.

It was probably the saddest Christmas I can remember.

Today, I can understand that dad was having a rough time trying to take care of a home, work a job, and raise five kids. I cannot imagine what he must have gone through having to deal with a wife who couldn't handle having children and five kids who had a mother who didn't want them. But it was Christmas Eve, for crying out loud.

Wait. I can imagine because I raised three sons by myself while working two or three jobs at a time. The only difference is I would have killed to protect my boys and stayed sober on Christmas Eve.

Dad had to have sighed with relief when mother left for the final time in 1951. His children were older now and needed less care. We were all in school and Kurt and Virginia had part-time jobs. My job had become taking care of the house. For one year I did all the cleaning, ironing, learned how to bake, and did most of the cooking. I took care of my younger brother and sister. I was twelve years old and I grew up fast.

We were living in Wisconsin when she left. Wisconsin had a law, at that time, that you had to wait one year before you could marry again.

Dad married my step-mom one year and one day after his divorce from my mother was final.

Hollyhocks

Our house in Kalispell was nice. It had a good-sized front porch to play on when it rained and a fenced-in back yard. There was also a wonderful crab apple tree whose limbs were perfect for climbing.

In the back of the house, there was a garage. An alley separated us from the houses behind us. The backyard was large and about one-fourth of it was a garden. As far back as I can remember, dad had a garden.

There wasn't a lot of yard on the right side of the house, but enough to run through to get to the back. Here, next to the house were these wonderful plants called Hollyhocks. I thought they were pretty when they bloomed. They showed off their pretty colors. I don't remember if there was a fragrance or not.

My dad would call them TOILET FLOWERS.

I never understood why he used that term until I started writing this book. Now I know why.

These flowers were at one time associated with outdoor bathrooms. They were perfect for blocking an unsightly outhouse. You didn't have to ask where the john was, you only had to look for the tall bell-shaped blooms.

Today the Hollyhock is a treasured garden beauty and the stinky reputation of these flowers has been long forgotten.

Chewing Tar

We did. When I lived in Kalispell, we chewed tar. In the summer, when the streets were being patched, we would find a glob of shiny black tar, wrap some of it around a stick, bite it off, and chew it like gum.

It tasted great and we never got sick from chewing it. Chewing tar back then was not unusual and there were a lot of different kinds. Road tar was what we chewed, but there was also roofing tar, spruce tar, pine tar, and a lot of others that people chewed.

I doubt it is the same today, so it is my solid recommendation not to try it. With all the chemicals used today, you might die and I don't want to be blamed.

Hair Care

Obviously, life in the Pare house wasn't rosy and wonderful. The turmoil between my parents had gone on for as long as I can remember. When mom would have enough of us kids and my dad, she would up and leave.

I've never been able to understand how a mother could leave her kids. The first couple of times she only left two kids behind. When she left for the third time, she had five kids wondering what the hell was happening.

Mom leaving meant that dad had to step in and take over her job plus his. I often wonder if dad took her back because he needed a babysitter and a cook more than he needed a wife.

We lived in Kalispell when she pulled her third disappearing act. I was in third grade at the time and could not understand why she had left. I remember a neighbor telling us that she had gone on a much-needed vacation to 'get away from you five brats'.

Dad hired a girl who would stay with us when he was on the road but when he was home, he did the housework and the cooking. He also made sure we went to church even though he didn't go with us.

I guess he also figured he was a barber.

It was time for me to have a haircut. He grabbed a little white stool and into the backyard we went. My hair was straight and all I needed was an inch cut off the ends. To hear him tell the story, I never held my head straight. Personally, I think the stool was crooked. As he finished up, he stepped back to check my new haircut out and decided one side needed to be 'evened out a little more'.

Then, the other side needed to be 'evened out'. This 'we need to even it out a little more' continued until he cut my hair to the middle of my ears.

The harder I cried, the more he swore. By the time he finished, I was the most pathetic-looking little girl you can imagine. It would have been better if he had put a bowl over my head. And left it there.

The next day I refused to go to school. Well, we sure weren't going to have any of that foolishness. So, off to school I went, wearing a purple scarf that I had folded in half like a triangle and wrapped around my head. I looked like Carmen Miranda without the fruit. I tied it in the front and left it on all day. Later that afternoon, my fourth-grade teacher, Mrs. Peterson, took me out in the hall and told me to take off the scarf. When she saw my hair she said, "Oh, my. Did your father do that on purpose or was it an accident?"

Today it would be called child abuse.

Wonder Cure

My brother, Kurt, was about eight or nine years old when he came down with an illness that totally stumped the doctors. Getting no help from any of the local doctors, my father finally took Kurt to Mayo Clinic to seek help.

Kurt was in pain for years. He suffered from abscesses mainly on his back, which my mother would tend to. He was frail and the disease stunted his growth and prevented him from turning his head from side to side.

It was eventually determined that Kurt had a disease known as actinomycosis. Although it was probably not true, it was said that he had chewed on a piece of grass that had been sprayed with some type of weed killer. I also remember hearing that they called this 'cows' disease'. Cows do and can get a form of actinomycosis.

After we moved to Kalispell, my parents found a doctor to treat my brother the best he could and try to keep him comfortable. And, then, da da – the wonder drug penicillin came to town. The doctor started treating Kurt with it and it worked. He was around twelve years old at the time.

Actinomycosis is a rare disease where bacteria spreads from one part of the body to another. Today, it is still being treated with penicillin.

Virginia also had bouts of illness throughout her youth. She suffered her first 'break down' when she was only in the fifth grade. She had rheumatic fever when she was in the 7th grade and another 'break down' when she was in the 8th grade.

I imagine having sick children only added to the stress of raising kids. Was this one of the reasons my parents couldn't get along? Probably. At least, Carol, George, and I made it through our growing-up years in pretty good health.

COLUMBUS, WISCONSIN

House in Columbus – About 2005

Riddledee, Diddledee!

Dad changed jobs again in 1949 and this change took the family back to Wisconsin. We moved to a small, wonderful town called Columbus. Dad lived there until he retired. I lived there until the day after I graduated from high school.

My father was Catholic and my mother, the daughter of a minister, was Lutheran. Religion can be a source of arguments in families and mine was no exception. My parents fought a lot about religion, which was strange to me at the time, as my father never went to church while he was married to my mother.

Although he allowed it, us three younger kids going to a parochial school was a thorn in his side. I went there from fifth to eighth grade. I received a religious education, plus the normal studies you have during those years. I didn't like going there because the 'cool' public school kids looked down on us. My dad also made fun of my grade school, which made me like it even less and I couldn't wait to get out of there and get 'cool'.

The school was a big, ugly two-story square building with four classrooms, four coatrooms (where you were sent when you were bad), and two bathrooms in the basement. There were two grades in each room and probably 25-35 kids in each room. There were always more kids in the 7th and 8th grade rooms. Some of the kids from public school transferred over during eighth grade to get their confirmation training. That old wooden building is still standing. It was converted into four apartments when the new Lutheran school was built. It actually looks better today than it did back then.

Picture – What old Luther School looks like in 2019. Converted to apartments.

When I was in the fifth grade, one of our homework assignments was to write a poem. I mentioned this at the supper table and my father told me he had a poem for me. After dinner, I wrote what he dictated and recited it the next day in front of the class.

Riddledee, diddledee, dumpdee;
The cat ran up the plum tree;
He ran so fast he scratched his ass;
And, never ran up the plum tree again.

After I finished reciting my poem and the kids stopped laughing, my teacher told me to go to the coatroom and stay there until school was over. My mother, who was unaware of what my father had done, had been called by my teacher and told to come and get me. She showed up after school. My father did not.

My mother saw no humor in this whatsoever and said she could never hold her head up in town again. My mother said that a lot.

Dad thought this hilarious and he laughed every time he told the story, and he told it a lot.

I was totally confused.

The Old Swimming Hole

My dad taught me how to swim and dive. Occasionally, we would drive to Lake Mills, have a picnic, and go swimming. He was a good swimmer but my mother was a fantastic swimmer. Sometimes, she would lie on her back and float for what seemed like forever. All you would see sticking out of the water is her face, boobs, and toes.

Columbus has a wonderful park called Fireman's Park. There is a large pavilion where parties, wedding dances, and gatherings took and still take place. The large building has been taken care of and is usually holding some type of affair every weekend.

In the early '50s, it had a community swimming pool. At some time, back then, someone decided it would be a really good idea to dig this enormous hole and fill it in with water and let their kids swim in it.

Picture - Columbus pool 1950

The bottom was like mud, of course. There was no filtration. It was a huge hole full of bacteria, urine, dead bugs, and God only knows what else. And, when the circus came to town, the elephants would drink the water.

On a warm summer day, we would walk to the park and go swimming. The pool was usually full of kids of all ages. I don't recall if there was a lifeguard but I've been told there was. I, also, don't recall anyone ever getting sick after playing in the mud hole. Miracles do happen.

Today, the town has a beautiful Aquatic Center for the enjoyment of its citizens. Of course, today you pay to play.

We got to play in the mud for free.

Picture – Aquatic Center in Columbus

<u>Switch Hitter</u>

My father's job took him on the road around three or four nights a week, so you would think he would have enjoyed being at home. But, nooo. He couldn't wait to shove his family in the car, get behind the wheel, and take a trip. To be fair, many of these trips were work-related, so he would try to combine them with some type of vacation.

I saw a lot of the country on these trips, back in the forties and fifties. In British Columbia, we traveled one-lane dirt roads heading for some sawmill. We would travel for miles and miles before we saw a house or a town. Every so often, would be a building where you could get gas or some food. They were called 50-mile house, 100-mile house, and so on. I never made it all the way to Alaska but came close when one summer dad drove to Prince Rupert in Canada.

We traveled west and north and, later on when he took real vacations, south to Florida. We never went east and we never flew. He drove and drove and drove.

We kids spent a lot of time riding in the back seat of the car. Cars back then didn't have air conditioning and, even when dad finally got a car with air, he wouldn't use it. You want air – open the windows.

Sometimes dad would spit a huge lugie out his window. It would usually find its way into the back seat of the car, via an open window. This was one of the few times we could yell at him and not get into trouble.

Seven people packed into a car during hot weather really sucked, especially as we got older and bigger. The place of honor in the car was the front seat between my mother and father. Which kid sat in this place of honor was decided by my mother. It was whoever might be her 'favorite child' at the time. We rotated as her moods changed and as we grew.

Picture – Five Pare Children
Virginia, Susan, Kurt
George and Carol 1950

The remaining four kids were crowded into the back seat where we couldn't stand being touched by each other. So, we did exactly that - we touched each other. Pretty soon, the 'stop it - stop touching me - ouch - cut it out' sounds would reach my father's ears. This was the signal he was waiting for. I don't know why we always did it, as we knew what would happen. Yet, we did it anyway. We were always so fricking bored.

Now the hunt was on. As he drove, he searched the side of the road looking for some nice young saplings growing along the highway. As soon as he found some, he would pull the car over to the side of the road and get out. The back seat was either deathly still at this point or we were fighting over whose fault it was that we were in trouble.

It usually took about ten seconds for dad to find the right switch. Out would come his pocketknife and he would cut a little branch to just the right size. Long enough to reach the backseat but short enough to fit across the visor. Then, looking at us to be sure we were watching, he would test it to make sure it had good flexibility. Without a word, he would get back into the car and place the switch above the visor. Now, I don't know if you have ever been hit with a willowy switch, but it hurts like hell. Seeing that switch up by the visor could keep us quiet for hours.

If we acted up again, this man - this switch hitter - would grab that switch with one hand and, without turning around or looking at us, he would land that hit directly on the right kid. And, we better not cry.

We found out at a very young age that you don't ever, ever whistle in the car while dad was driving. At some time in my dad's life, a passenger had whistled in his car and he got a flat tire. When it happened the second time, whistling was forbidden. He was funny superstitious like that.

With the exception of the historical marker signs on the side of the highways, we never saw any touristy things driving from point A to point B. Dad had a time schedule and he stuck to it. The markers did not cost anything to read, though, and dad would pull over and stop so we could read them. We knew that we better read fast because a few minutes were all we were given to absorb some history and we were back on the road.

I learned a lot about Lewis and Clark, Sacagawea, and the Continental Divide during those trips.

We learned to entertain ourselves while traveling those thousands of miles. There were no electronic games to play with or cell phones. We read a lot, took naps, and stared out the window. And, we touched each other.

<u>Wannigan</u>

When Dad was on the road for business, he stayed in a hotel and ate his meals in restaurants. He had an expense account.

When we were all traveling with him, we stayed in cabins. When I was a kid, there were no motels. You would drive until you found some cabins that were usually located on the outskirts of a town or set back off the road in the woods, miles from nowhere.

Now, by definition, a wannigan is a small chest, which holds provisions for a camp or cabin. Dad's wannigan was nothing more than a cardboard box. This box was placed strategically in the trunk for easy access. It held all the supplies needed to make coffee, utensils, cereal, glass coffee cups, mustard, mayonnaise, and various items deemed necessary for survival.

After ten to twelve hours of driving, to get wherever the hell we were going now, dad would start to look for a cabin where we could spend the night. The cabin always had a small kitchenette and enough beds to hold six people. Yes, one cabin for six people. I usually wound up sleeping in the back seat of the car. On some occasions, George would have to join me – him in the front seat and me in the back. Some of those nights got pretty darn cold and we would shiver ourselves to sleep.

Usually, dad found a grocery store before he found a cabin where we would spend the night. He would buy some milk for our breakfast cereal, and bread and lunch meat for sandwiches that we would eat the next day.

Sometimes, he would stop and buy some cold pop before we ate our lunch. Therefore, we might have some pop with our lunchmeat sandwiches that were made with bread that was loaded with MAYONNAISE that had been sitting in the car in the wannigan for the entire trip. There was no cooler in our car – only a cardboard box dad called a wannigan. We should all have died from food poisoning.

Bathroom breaks were special. After practically dying from holding it in for miles, dad would finally pull over so we could pee. We'd jump out of the car, run down the ditch beside the road, and head to the woods to pull down our pants, squat, and pee. One time when I was running into the woods, I got tangled up in some rusty old barbwire that was on the ground. My ankle was torn up real bad. Good thing we had some bandages in that wannigan to fix me up. I still have the scar. Of course, my brothers had an advantage, being able to stand up to pee. My mother, however, was the best. She would sit on the running board, pull her panties to the side, and pee right there.

Traveling became tolerable after my older brother and sister were out of school and went off to do their thing. Actually, life, in general, became better. Now there were only five of us in the car and there was more room in the back seat. The switch no longer appeared by the visor. Gas stations became our bathrooms instead of the woods. Sometimes bologna sandwiches would be ham sandwiches, but there were always homemade sandwiches of some kind for lunch. We never stopped at a restaurant or a fast-food place to eat lunch. On extremely rare occasions, when dad couldn't find a cabin, we stayed in a hotel.

I looked out the windows when we traveled. I saw mountain sheep walking on cliffs and whitetail deer running in woods. I saw an occasional moose watching us as we traveled in their world and we fed bears out of car windows.

I watched glacier-filled rivers go by and I drank pure, cold water out of fast-moving streams. I saw canyons with colors only God could paint and I walked in the snow on mountaintops in July. I saw beauty beyond belief in a country that has no equal.

I watched the world go by from the window in the back seat of a car.

We sent postcards to our friends, which they would get after we got back home. And, sometimes, when mom liked me best for the day, I got to sit in the front seat.

Dad never stopped driving. He continued to drive until he died at the age of eighty-seven. Even then, he was planning his hunting trip to Wyoming. He couldn't wait to pack his wannigan and go. After he died, my step-mom told me that she was sad he was gone, but at least she didn't have to ride in a car anymore. She was happy she could finally stay home and not have to travel again. And, she didn't.

She never learned to drive a car. My dad never had a car accident. Neither of them ever flew in an airplane.

The Games People Played

When the street lights went on, it was time to go home. When you got home, you played outside until your mother yelled at you to get in the house.

During the summer months, we play out of doors as long as we could. We played games like Hide and Seek, Red Light-Green Light, Mother May I, Marbles, and Simon Says.

I loved to roller skate on the sidewalks and kept the key on a string around my neck.

Picture – Roller-skates with a key

When the weather was bad or rainy, we played games at the kitchen table. Canasta was big back in the early '50s. So were Checkers and Monopoly. My grandparents had a game called Chinese Checkers that was completely different from Checkers. It was played with a bunch of marbles.

George had a train set he played with and we girls played Pick up Sticks and Jacks. Carol played dolls with her baby dolls. I did not play with dolls.

When I was in seventh or eighth grade, dad bought our first TV. Even though we would watch a lot of shows on TV, we still played our games.

Our yard was small, so Davies Park, which was only a house away from ours, was our playground where we played baseball.

I consider myself lucky that we didn't have cell phones back then. You could be gone for hours and no one could check up on you.

If we wanted to talk to someone, we used a landline phone. Dad had a phone in his office and there was an extension phone in an upstairs bedroom. We had a private line because it was a business phone. Our phone number was 135.

Some people had a party line, which was common back in the '40s and '50s. A party line was shared by more than one family and there was no privacy at all. If you were talking on the phone, anyone on your party line could pick up their phone and listen in. If you had an emergency and someone on your party line was talking, you had the right to tell them to hang up so you could make a call for help. People who had a party line would know if a call was for them by how many times their phone rang.

We called a lot of people we didn't know and pranked them. "Do you have Prince Albert in a can?" we would ask the person who answered the phone at the drugstore. When they said yes, we would tell them to let him out. And, then we'd hang up and laugh and laugh. "Is your refrigerator running?" was another one that we thought was hysterically funny. We were young kids doing what kids do.

Back in the '50s, you didn't have to lock your doors or worry about your kids walking from one end of town to the other and being raped or murdered. It was a wonderful, peaceful little town where the adults ruled and kids listened. We grew up respecting our elders – and, perhaps, fearing them a little. Whatever the case – it worked!

Be Careful What You Ask For

I never wanted a piano, but my mother did. My mother was probably one of the most talented persons I ever knew. She excelled at everything she attempted. She was raised in a home where music was a staple. She played the piano and the organ and she had a beautiful singing voice.

When she decided that she wanted a piano, my dad said no. He said it was too expensive and they couldn't afford it. I thought my mother had forgotten about it until I was approaching my eleventh birthday.

"Tell your father you want a piano for your birthday. Tell him you want to take piano lessons. Don't tell him I told you to ask him," she said to me.

I didn't want to take piano lessons. I finally asked dad if I could have a piano for my birthday to get my mother off my back. My dad wasn't stupid. He knew what was going on. He looked at me and said, "We'll see."

I went about my business, totally forgetting about any old piano. When I came home from school, on the day of my birthday, I saw a truck backed up to the porch. Dad and five men were unloading an old upright piano.

What the frick! I was getting a piano for my birthday. Now, I was going to have to take piano lessons.

I hated every lesson I had on that $50.00, eighteen-ton, upright piano. I had my hands slapped by the teacher for making mistakes and couldn't wait to quit. I learned to play but I was never very good. The lessons continued until I was in high school and I was finally allowed to quit.

Carol and George took piano lessons for years. Both became excellent pianists.

Picture - Kurt, Virginia, Susan, and Carol
George – First Christmas after mother left.

When my son, Perry, was three years old, he sat down at that piano and plunked out a tune. That's when I knew he would be taking lessons and, to this day, he plays a mean piano.

I think the fact that I received a piano after asking for one, and my mother didn't, pretty much tells the story of their marriage. My parents were divorced a year after my eleventh birthday.

I Have a What?

It was the winter of 1949, we were living in Columbus, and I was in the fifth grade. One night dad got a phone call, which was kind of unusual. Dad was on the phone a lot when he was working at home, but he didn't get a lot of calls at night. Ten minutes later he was still talking and each time we came close enough to hear him, he shooed us away.

After that phone call was over, mother and dad sequestered themselves behind closed office doors for what seemed like forever. When they came out, they told all of us to go sit down in the living room, they had something to tell us.

Dad had a brother we had never heard about—which meant we had an uncle. This man had a couple of kids which meant we had a couple of cousins. We knew that dad's father had been killed in a logging accident before he was two. His mother died about a year later when he was around three years old. Dad had been raised in Peshtigo by George and Suzie Albrecht, who had no children of their own. What we didn't know was that dad had a younger brother who, after their parents died, wound up living with a dirt-poor family who had gobs of kids. Dad had been raised with all the benefits and was spoiled rotten and his brother's life was shit. They had lost contact with each other when they were still young.

We were told that there had been a horrible car accident in Texas and my uncle was severely injured and not expected to live. He had sustained a serious head injury, had lost an eye, had multiple broken bones, internal injuries, and had a blood clot in his brain. Our cousins were Betty, who was six, and George (aka Bunny), who was five. The local authorities had spent days trying to find a relative and had finally tracked down dad. They told him that someone needed to come get these two kids.

Mother said she was going to Texas to get them and bring them back. Which she did. She hopped on the next train out of town and away she went to Texas. She picked up these two little kids who had traveled around the country with their father while he worked odd jobs. They had no home. They had lived on a reservation or out of cars most of their lives and had never been to school. They thought their mother was dead but weren't really sure.

Seven days later my mother got off the train with those two little kids in tow.

The only time we saw any Blacks or Mexicans in town was during the canning season when they came to town to work at the canning factory. So, when Betty and Bunny showed up it was the talk of the town. These kids were half American-Indian but they looked full-blooded. They had been raised on a reservation until their mom disappeared. It was assumed that if they were Indians, well then - so were all the Pares. For the next few months, we were fodder for gobs of racial jokes that no one got into trouble for.

Early spring a strange man showed up at our door. It was my Uncle George, who scared the shit out of me all the while he lived with us. The accident had scarred him a lot and I don't think I ever talked to him. I stayed away from him as much as possible. He was always asking my father to buy him cigarettes, which was a big deal and caused a lot of fights between him and my dad.

Picture - Cousins Betty and George (Bunny)
with Carol in front of Columbus House

On a day that dad was out of town on business, Uncle George left the house with Betty and Bunny. I watched him walk down the street towards town carrying suitcases. I told my mother and she told me to follow him but "don't let him see you". I followed them, playing detective, sneaking from tree to tree. I watched them go to the bus station, get on a bus, and then they were gone.

Just like that. Gone.

I've always wondered where Uncle George got the money for the bus tickets.

A good thirty years later, dad and I were having a conversation when he mentioned his brother. He said that he hoped his brother had a will and left him some money when he died. He was still waiting to be reimbursed for the cost of taking care of him and his kids and for all those cigarettes he bought for him.

He was still waiting when he passed away. I don't believe he ever heard from his brother again.

Montana Summers

I had finished fifth grade. The car trunk was packed full of suitcases, Of course, the wannigan was in exactly the right place in the trunk for easy access. Dad had rented a house for the summer on Flathead Lake, a few miles outside of Somers, Montana. This house was next to the house we had lived in when my youngest brother, George, was born.

This was the best summer I had as a child.

The owners of this house had converted the detached garage into a huge bedroom and this is where we three girls slept. My youngest sister, Carol, was only seven and she was usually afraid to stay out there. It probably was because someone scared the shit out of her with stories of bears breaking in and monsters looking through the windows. Even if she started out sleeping in the garage, seven nights out of ten she wound up back in the house.

To get to the lake, all we had to do was cross the road, go down a steep hill, and jump in. Every day, for almost three months, I lived in the water. Occasionally, my oldest brother and I would row the boat to Somers. Sometimes, we would hop on our bikes and ride the three miles to go to the store or get the mail.

Flathead Lake was beautiful back in 1949. It is a huge glacier-fed lake and it was cold. There were few homes in that area back then. I hear that has changed now and it is a busy vacation area with big, beautiful, expensive houses.

It was this summer that my parents hired Anna Lou Oursland to take care of us while they traveled to Alaska. She became our substitute mother for almost eight weeks. Behave, listen to Anna Lou, and stay out of trouble was all dad said, and away they went.

We had a ball. We laughed, we swam, we rode our bikes, ate a lot of peanut butter and jelly sandwiches, and slept like babies after playing in the water for half the day. We enjoyed ourselves like never before. Or, since. Things that were barely funny became hysterical and we would laugh our asses off.

Yes, it was the best summer ever.

A close second came the following year. We stayed in Whitefish that summer right on the lake. This time dad rented a huge cabin that could sleep all of us and was right on the water. We spent most days playing in the water and being lazy.

It wasn't as much fun as the year before, as Virginia was sick but it was still a nice way to spend my summer.

After that, we stayed home during the summer months. It was the end of long summer vacations living on lakes and riding bikes through the Montana countryside.

Birds and Bunnies

When I was twelve years old, I asked dad if we could have a dog. He said no and don't ask again. He made it extremely clear, to the entire family, that there would be no dogs or cats in our home. 'Don't ask again' meant precisely that.

Therefore, we were shocked when dad walked into the house one day carrying a cage and a box with a bird in it. He had been in Milwaukee on business, had stopped at a pet store, and bought a budgie bird. We named him Pete and he was our second pet. Like most dumb birds, Pete sat around all day and ate. He didn't sing like a canary - he simply made noise. He never learned how to talk. Dad started clipping his wings after we had trouble catching him when he flew around the house. After that, he fell on the floor and we'd pick him up and put him back in his cage.

One day when I came home from school, I noticed a lot of activity coming from Pete's cage. Dad had found a baby robin in the yard. He put it in the cage with Pete to give him some company. Pete also had a mouse drop by one day to say hello. Needless to say, both visits were short-lived.

Pete was with us for about four years. When he got sick, dad euthanized him. A coffee can and a little ether was all it took.

Sometimes, I wish they made people-sized coffee cans.

In 1955, dad announced that we would be going to Montana over our Easter vacation. By now, Carol, George, and I were the only ones living at home. We were taking the train out west. Dad was going to pick up a new company car and drive it back home. This trip was probably the best trip we ever had. The train ride was great and dad was the most laid-back I ever saw him.

Picture -Dad and Florence (She was the best stepmother ever.)

We kids must have been getting on dad's nerves on the drive home because we sure getting on each other's. We were going through some town in Montana when, suddenly, he pulled the car over and parked. Stay in the car was all he said, as he walked away. After what seemed like forever, he returned carrying a good-sized cardboard box. He opened the back door of the car and handed the box to George.

Inside that box was the cutest little white bunny. After many hours of extensive debate, we decided to name him Bugs. Aren't all rabbits called Bugs kinda like all parakeets are called Pete? That night we took him into the motel room with us, with instructions to keep him in the box. George decided to let Bugs sleep with him and Bugs peed the bed. And, of course, he was yelled at for that. My brother – not Bugs.

Bugs never lived inside the house with us. After we got home, dad built him a large pen. Half of the pen was open but covered with chicken wire and half was enclosed to keep him out of the elements. Dad would move that pen from one area of the lawn to the other and Bugs would eat the grass. Sometimes, dad would let us bring him into the house and my step-mom would give him a bath in the kitchen sink.

Bugs got big pretty fast. He lasted with our family until the weather started to turn cold. I came home from school one day and Bugs was gone. Dad said he gave him to a woman that raised rabbits, but I noticed that the can of ether was missing from the shelf in the garage.

I do believe the chicken we had for dinner that night looked and tasted a little strange. Just kidding. I mean, like, we certainly didn't eat Bugs. Or, did we?

Note: The first pet we had was a bunny. Dad got him when we lived in Kalispell back in 1947. He didn't last long. A neighbor's cat killed him in the backyard.

Easter Chicken

Why is there an Easter Bunny,
And not an Easter Chicken?
It doesn't make much sense to me,
And I've done a lot of thinkin'.

It's the chicken that lays the eggs,
That the kids get on Easter morn.
Yet the rabbit gets all the credit,
For those chicks that won't be born.

The poor chicken leads a sorry life,
All cooped up for just one reason.
To lay those eggs we eat each day,
And even more during Easter season.

Now we all know the bunny's cuter,
Then a chicken will ever be.
But, to give him all the credit,
Just doesn't seem right to me.

So, when Easter comes around this year,
In tribute to all the chickens -
It won't be a ham sittin' on our table,
Nope, it's a chicken leg we'll be pickin'.

Play Ball!

I guess there's an unwritten rule that dads are supposed to teach their sons how to throw a ball. It makes no difference what kind of a ball. The seasons usually dictate if it is a baseball, a basketball, or a football that is going to be tossed around. Fathers are supposed to play catch with their sons. This ritual is probably more for the father so he can show off to his son how good he is at throwing a ball.

Let's take throwing a baseball for example. It's a Saturday afternoon and the family has finished lunch. Mom tells dad to take their son out and play with him for a while so she can get some peace and quiet. The son whines he doesn't want to but dad tells him to go outside so they can 'toss the ball around'. Dragging his feet, the little boy goes outside.

It starts out well enough. The father shows the kid where to stand and how to hold his hands. Then, he gently throws the ball to his son and, of course, it lands at the son's feet. The son looks at the ball. Then he looks at his father. The dad tells him to pick it up and throw it back to him. The little boy picks it up and throws it back to the dad, where it lands two feet away from the kid. He stands there looking at the ball until Dad says to pick it up and throw it again. He picks up the ball and this time he throws it into the flowerbed next to him. Dad says throw it again. The ball winds up in the road barely missing a passing car. Dad goes into the street, picks up the ball, walks to his son, and hands it to him. The boy then drops the ball. Dad then says to try again and the kid picks it up and throws the ball behind him. This scenario is repeated over and over for the next ten minutes, the ball never even getting close to the father, while the father's kind encouraging words to his son turn to crap.

"See, this is how it's done. No – you need to hold the ball like this. Keep your hands together. Keep your feet apart. Watch me, I'll show you. Try it again. One more time, you'll get it. Try the other hand. You almost got it that time. Good try. Try throwing it overhand, like this. Never mind, just do what you were doing. You need to jump up to catch it. Watch me! I said watch me! You need to look at the ball. You're not doing it right! What's wrong with you? Two hands – you need to use both hands! You catch like a girl! God, you're so clumsy! No, you can't quit! What? You're going to cry now? You're such a baby!"

It makes no difference what kind of a ball it is – the kid is going to get hurt. Dad will get frustrated because Billy sucks and he will start to throw that ball a little harder and faster and little Billy will get it in the face. And, cry. He will go running into the house to his mother screaming, "Daddy hurt me." Mommy, being the great mother she is, will immediately run to the door and yell at her husband, "Why'd you have to throw that ball so hard? What's wrong with you? When are you going to learn he's a little boy? God, you're so stupid! I don't know why I even married you."

Dad, who is already pissed at his sucky kid, will throw the ball on the ground and go across the street to have a beer with his neighbor, who is sitting on the curb shaking his head. He has spent the last hour trying to teach his daughter how to roller skate and she is now in the house crying.

And, little Billy will smile and go off to his room to play his games, which is what he wanted to be doing all along.

My father played catch a lot with my younger brother and me, even though I'm a girl. We would play catch in the street. Dad never did make me cry, although I'm not sure about my brother. He probably didn't make him cry either because if we were playing catch that meant he was in a good mood. He told me that I had a better arm on me than most boys. This was a real compliment coming from dad. I think he wished I had been a boy.

Dads and kids throwing balls around is a good bonding experience and we were always grateful when our dad would spend some time with us. It's amusing that the only time a neighbor's window got broken was because of a wild ball thrown by my dad.

I raised three sons and I was the one who played catch with them when they were young. I used to love throwing the ball around with my boys. What was especially cool was, when they got a little older, they gave me Mothers' Day cards and Fathers' Day cards.

Ticks

My father was probably the happiest when he was in the woods. When he was barely a teenager, he trapped in the woods around Peshtigo. He checked those traps every morning, hoping to find some type of animal. Pelts from animals, such as beaver, fox, and muskrats brought good money, while squirrels and rabbits helped put food on the table.

The Iron Mountain, Michigan area (located in Michigan's Upper Peninsula) was one of my father's favorite places to hunt. Nestled deep in the woods, some miles away from Iron Mountain, was a hunting lodge where the same men gathered for years to hunt.

Picture – Dad on right – Hunting Lodge

Dad started hunting there when he was a teenage boy, back in the early 1920s. My father took us to this lodge on many occasions. However, by then it had been updated and another log cabin – the mess hall - had been built. So, it now boasted of having two buildings. Whoops – three buildings. I almost forgot the outhouse. The bunkhouse held enough bunk beds to sleep around ten to twelve men. The wood stove would usually burn out during the night and by morning the water in the washbasins would be frozen solid.

The mess hall had heat via a fireplace and this is where the men spent most of their time when not sleeping or hunting. They ate there, drank there, and told the same stories over and over about their hunting skills. It was also there that they took the ticks off their bodies that had decided to settle in for a long winter's stay. Sometimes, the ticks would burrow so deep into the hunters' bodies that they had to hold a flame over that area to get the ticks to back out. I hate ticks. My father removed more than one from my body when I was little.

My father continued to hunt in that area long after the hunting group disbanded. We would always go there in early fall so he could get his blind ready for hunting season. We would hike far into the woods and find his blind from the year before. Then, he would repair it, camouflage it, and get it ready for the coming hunting season.

Blueberries and Bears

One of the things the Upper Peninsula is known for is its wild blueberries. Today, there are many areas open to the public where you can go to pick wild blueberries. Besides blueberries being there – there are bears. And, bears love blueberries.

It was blueberry season. We were going berry picking.

Dad drove down a long dusty old road into the woods. When the road ended, he stopped the car and told us all to get out. He opened the trunk and handed each of us a small metal bucket with a handle on it. Away we all went, into the countryside, to pick blueberries. It was hot out, the grass was dry and had turned brown. We walked until we started to find blueberries growing on the side of a hill.

"You pick until you fill your bucket and I better not catch you eating any of them," dad said to us.

We had picked for some time when my older brother, Kurt, grabbed my youngest brother's pail and started banging it against his. He yelled 'bear', thinking he had seen a bear by some trees and that the noise would scare the bear away.

Our picking had scattered us to different locations on that dry dusty hill, but when he yelled, we all headed toward dad. Or, rather, where we had last seen dad. He wasn't there. Run to the car – run to the car – we all yelled and made tracks in that direction.

My brother continued banging the two pails together as he ran, while my younger brother and sister were screaming in fear. As we ran our pails were swinging and blueberries were falling out all over the

85

place. We were sure that a bear was chasing us. We were scared to death and afraid we'd be killed.

We reached the car (without anyone actually being mauled or killed) and there was my father in the front seat – sound asleep. We stopped short and looked at each other. Experience had taught us that waking up dad could be painful.

So, we didn't actually wake him. We merely made enough noise so that he woke up. There is a difference.

When we told him how a bear was trying to kill us and how my brother had saved us from clanging the buckets together, he laughed.

Well, he laughed until he found out we had lost most of the blueberries. Then, he gave us that 'I'm not kidding look', which always scared the bejesus out of us, and said, "GO PICK THEM UP!"

The Green Couch

For years now I have had this habit of sleeping on the couch when I don't feel well. I want to throw an afghan over myself and curl up and stay there until I get better. I've decided that I do this because I don't want to die in my bed.

Now, if I'm going to die, why wouldn't I want to be already laid out in bed when they find me? They can throw me on a gurney and carry me away. I sleep almost naked, so the undertaker wouldn't even have much to remove. Then be sure to burn the mattress, 'cause you know why and that should take care of that.

Then recently, it hit me. That's not the reason at all.

Until I was fifteen, I had to share a bedroom. In Kalispell, I shared one with both Virginia and Carol. When we moved to Columbus, I shared a room with Carol. Eventually, Virginia moved out and I got that room.

If I got sick while I was sharing a room, I spent that time on the couch in the living room so I wouldn't infect anyone. That was almost like being on vacation. I would sleep most of the day and try to spend the night watching TV turned down low so no one else could hear it. I usually fell asleep and then woke up when the 'Star-Spangled Banner' played at midnight. TV stations were usually on until midnight back then. They all played the National Anthem before signing off.

If I was running a fever dad would make me a drink out of whiskey, boiling hot water, and lemon juice, and make me drink it down. It would make me sweat out a fever and cure a cough. Years later, when I made a mixture for my boys, it was equal parts of honey, lemon juice, and whiskey given to them on a teaspoon. In 1962, Perry was a baby with a bad cold when that remedy was recommended by his doctor.

The only couch I remember is a green one. We had that couch when we lived in Kalispell. Back then we called it a davenport. Dad had that couch when he retired. It went with him when he moved to Stone Lake. At that time, it had to have been at least thirty-five years old. When he moved back to Columbus, the couch did not. It never wore out.

Perhaps the reason I still hit the couch and want to stay there when I don't feel good is that, in my head, couch equals feeling better.

Well, Fork Me

Like most families, we ate our meals in the kitchen. The dining room was reserved for special occasions and holidays. Dinner was at 6:00 p.m. sharp. Once we moved to Columbus, we had assigned seating at the kitchen table. When dad was home, I sat next to him on his left side.

Everyone sat in a chair except me. I sat on a white stool that I pulled up to the table before I sat down for meals. After Virginia moved out, I got her chair but I still had to sit next to dad.

Manners became more important as we grew older. Nothing would be passed if we didn't add 'please' to 'pass whatever' and we had darn well better be sure we said thank you. We never helped ourselves to a second helping without asking first. If there was a pork chop left on the platter, we knew better than to reach for it. It belonged to dad. We never took - we asked.

And, yes, we could not leave the table until our plates were clean. There were times that George fell asleep while still sitting at the table long after the rest of us had finished our meal.

I hated my mother every time she made chop suey. I hated it, she knew I hated it and I had to eat it. I gagged getting it down and always threw up immediately after eating it.

I was more of a meat and potato girl, but I could easily make a meal out of only potatoes. Especially, baked potatoes. I loved them.

Sitting next to dad was a dangerous business. If you ever, and I mean ever, rested an elbow on the table while you were eating, you were forked. Usually, it was in the arm, but any part of the body that was within reach could and would be stabbed. He never drew blood, but many times those indentations left from the tines of the forks took a long time to disappear. At one time or the other, every kid got it. As I sat so close to dad, I was forked a lot.

I used to tell my kids to take their elbows off the table and I've been known occasionally fork them – just for fun.

Six Pack Sue

We had one small bookcase in our home in Columbus. It had three shelves and it held three books - *Hiawatha, Grimm's Fairy Tales, Volumes I and II* - and a few knick-knacks. It also held copies of the National Geographic magazine.

Today this magazine is not considered porn. Back in the '50s – well, let's say it's the closest to it our house ever saw. My oldest brother couldn't wait for the next issue to arrive so he could check it out. He saw pictures of tits from all over the world. I don't think dad cared, but if my stepmother mentioned these pictures to my dad, the magazine would disappear forever.

When dad was in town, he would drive to the post office to get the mail. He usually left about the same time we left the house to walk to school, which was a good hike from where we lived. We probably did have to walk a mile or more but at least it wasn't uphill both ways. It could be freezing cold, raining, snowing, or a tornado pending – but he never gave us a ride to school. We walked.

The one exception was when I was a senior in high school and I broke my foot playing basketball. It was in the middle of winter, and I was on crutches for six weeks. He paid my boyfriend $25.00 to pick me up and take me to school. That was huge.

I started smoking when I was fourteen and probably started drinking not long after that. When I was a junior in high school, one of my nicknames was 'six-pack Sue'. I never went home drunk, never got caught, and never got in trouble. Once or twice dad mentioned that I smelled like smoke and I would say that kids were smoking in the car. He had smoked for years so it probably wouldn't have been a big deal if he knew I smoked.

The only thing to do in that town at night, anyway, was to pick up a six-pack, ride around town or go and park somewhere and drink beer and neck. "Six-pack Sue" should have been "a beer or two Sue" as I don't think I ever drank a six-pack all by myself.

Dad stopped smoking when he was about fifty-five or so. He smoked around two packs a day and he quit cold turkey. A few years later he made my step-mom quit, although she only smoked one or two cigarettes a day. I stopped after fifty years of smoking – also cold turkey. I loved smoking and it is probably the only thing I ever did really well. It was unbelievably easy for me to quit. I never picked up another cigarette or was tempted to smoke again after that.

I think sweets did the trick. I didn't need a cigarette but I needed a cookie.

In 1986, after being married to an alcoholic for a while, I stopped drinking. I don't mind anyone having a drink or two but most people don't stop at two. I've seen firsthand what drinking can do to a family and it isn't pleasant.

I think they should totally legalize pot and bring prohibition back or, at least, make it a two-drink limit country.

Bowling and Driving

The old bowling alley in Columbus was a great place to hang out, bowl a few games, and drink a few beers. I think it had about twelve alleys but I could be mistaken. It's a brewery now. A new bowling alley opened up on the outskirts of town.

Dad was a good bowler. He was in a league but quit a few years after he married Florence.

I never bowled with my dad. I wish I had because I'm pretty sure I would have beaten his ass.

I started bowling when I was a junior in high school. I was good. I averaged between 150 to 200 a game. The highest score I ever bowled was 287. I never made a 300 game.

I worked at the bakery in town while I was in my last two years of high school. Most of my money went to pay for my bowling. I had a friend who would bowl with me but never had any money, so I usually paid for her, too.

The bowling alley became our hangout for a while. I started drinking beer there when I was seventeen. When I turned eighteen and showed the bartender my ID, they were more than a little ticked off.

I didn't get a driver's license when I turned sixteen, like most kids. Dad's only car was a company car and we were not allowed to drive it.

Ray taught me to drive after we were married. I passed my driver's test the first time trying.

I've been driving for fifty-four years and I have never got a ticket. Mostly because I wasn't caught doing something wrong. Well, I was stopped for speeding once in Wisconsin but the lady cop let me go. She said she didn't want to be the one to spoil my perfect driving record.

Lucked out that time.

Mashed Potatoes and Pumpkin Pie

The sun is not shining this Thanksgiving morn,
The weather is rainy, gloomy and gray.
People are traveling in cars and in planes
To see loved ones who live far, far away.

Our table has been set with the best china today;
Just polished silverware has been carefully laid.
Fresh linen napkins are being used for a change;
And, fall flowers in vases are being displayed.

There are fresh pumpkin pies just starting to cool;
Tom turkey is stuffed and looking quite brown.
The wonderful smells of this day fill the home;
And, dad just came back from going to town.

You can tell he's already downed a few drinks,
By the way he walks and talks and his smell.
Mom looks aghast with fear in her eyes and
Knows that this dinner is headed for hell.

The guests that have come to share in this meal
Get up from the table and walk out the door.
Dad's just thrown his plate against the wall,
Fallen off of his chair and passed out on the floor.

The sun's still not shining this Thanksgiving day;
Mom's cleaned up the mess and the dishes are done.
But all I can think of as I sit in my room,
Is that Christmas is coming and it sure won't be fun.

Picture – Arthur Pare with a big buck

Tinsel Time

The end of November meant dad was gone deer hunting in northern Wisconsin. Dad never missed deer hunting. I cannot remember him ever coming home without at least one deer tied to the front of his car and a tree tied on the top. The tree would stay on the porch until the day before Christmas. Then the fun began.

Christmas Eve Day – No plans were to be made for that day and all children living in the home were to be present and accounted for. If you were too young to participate, you had to sit on the couch and observe and learn. Someday you would be the ball mover and a tree tinsel decorator and it was important that you knew the exact steps of how to accomplish these chores.

After lunch was over and the dishes were done, everyone would assemble in the sitting room. Dad would then pick one of us to go outside to help him ready the tree for admittance into our home.

The Tree - The first step was to get the tree to fit into the house and the base of the tree to fit into the stand. Dad's eye was pretty good so, when he picked out his trees in the woods, they usually fit height-wise and very little trimming was needed on the top of the tree. Sometimes, a few branches needed to be cut off the bottom near the trunk. Once the trunk was trimmed to fit into the base, the tree would be brought into the house and set in place. The tree was always placed in the formal living room, in front of a window, so everyone could see our tree as they drove or walked by.

Usually, some type of spruce was dad's choice but we did have some nice pines. Of course, being a real tree, it was placed in water to keep it fresh. The water was replenished daily until the tree came down. This would be when most of the needles were noticeably gone. If a tree still looked good, it stayed up. It not only stayed up – it stayed lit. On Valentine's Day in 1956, friends at school asked me, "Hey, Pare, when the hell is your old man going to take his Christmas tree down?"

There was one time that dad brought home three trees. He put up all three and decorated them. It actually was kind of cool.

Stringing the lights – During the time the tree lights had been put away and getting them out of the box a year later, the lights always managed to be tangled up. There had to be goblins playing in the attic while we were sleeping. Getting these lights untangled always took a long time and was definitely the worse phase of the tree-trimming process.

We did not have cute little lights that twinkled. We had lights with big bulbs that screwed in and if one blew out the entire string quit working. Before the lights could be put on the tree, they needed to be checked. This meant that if the lights did not go on each bulb would be removed from its socket, one at a time. A new bulb would be screwed in and, if the lights still didn't go on, the new bulb would be removed and the old bulb would be screwed back in. This continued until we found the culprit and all the lights were glowing. Process of elimination. It was rare, indeed, for the lights to be working the first time they were plugged in and this process was time-consuming. Once all the lights were working properly, my father would then string the lights on the tree while we sat and watched him. By now, he was normally in a bad mood.

Placing the balls – We used the same balls on the tree forever. They were glass balls and they broke easily. Except for the star on top, there was never anything else on our trees, like mementos or stuff us kids made at school. Only balls. Dad would place each ball on the tree while we sat and watched him. Then he would sit down and study the tree to decide if a ball needed to be moved a little to the right or to the left, or up or down. If a ball was to be moved, we were now intelligent enough, with his direction, to move it to its new location. This continued until all the balls on the tree had been perfectly placed to his satisfaction.

Tinsel – Although we reused most of the tinsel from the previous year, Dad would buy a few new boxes of tinsel for the tree. Whatever siblings still living at home and old enough to take direction, would take a handful of tinsel and place each strand on the tree - one by one - as dad told us where to place them. He would sit on the couch and tell us where to put each frickin' piece of tinsel.

Once the tree was decorated and the mess cleaned up, we were told to leave the room and stay out. The two pocket doors to the room were closed.

We always opened our gifts on Christmas Eve. Santa would come while we were at church and, when we got home, the doors to the living room would be open and the gifts would be under the tree. Dad was usually in a better mood than he had been when we left for church. It was after five and he'd had his first cocktail. We still weren't allowed in the living room.

Opening the gifts - For some reason, even though we had eaten before church, we now had to have a snack before we were allowed into the living room. This accomplished, we could go to our assigned seats in the living room. Each one of us had a pile of gifts under the tree and dad would hand them out. No two people ever opened a gift at the same time. After a gift was opened, it would be passed around so everyone could examine it and oohhh and aahhh. Then dad would have another glass of wine. He didn't have to go far to refill his glass. There was always a jug sitting on the floor next to him. Ten minutes could pass between opening a gift and the next person's turn.

If a gift was tied up with a string or ribbon, it was jackknife time. You got off your chair and took the gift to dad so he could use his jackknife to cut the string. The more glasses of wine he'd had, the more that jackknife swung around. To this day, I don't know why someone wasn't stabbed.

We never received a lot of stuff at Christmas and our gifts were mostly practical things like clothes. I did get matching luggage as gifts two years in a row and I received some perfume one year. I don't remember one other gift I ever received.

Carol usually cried with happiness after opening every one of her gifts, so that wasted even more time. My brothers and I usually spent this time making fun of her dramatics.

Three hours or so later, this ritual would finally be over and the jug would be empty.

Bullying

I cannot remember one kid that I went to school with that decided to end their life because they were being picked on. It may have happened somewhere, but it sure didn't happen in the fifties in Columbus. Our parents would have killed us for being so stupid.

When some smart-ass kid called me a name, usually a boy, I gave it right back to them. I didn't go home and curl up into a ball and decide life was no longer worth living. Name-calling was mostly done in grade school. Once we hit high school, the name-calling pretty much came to an end.

There was no bullying. If a couple of guys had a beef, they settled it off the school grounds and that was the end of it. My friends and I had lots of nicknames for the nerds and weird kids, but we never said it to their faces. We kept it between us and no one got hurt. Nobody knocked my books to the floor, bumped into me in the hallway between classes, or wrote nasty notes.

First, we were raised to respect each other. Second, our teachers and principal would never have allowed it and, third, if our parents found out the shit would have hit the fan.

FEAR. Let's face it. We were raised in fear. If we got into trouble in school, the parents backed the teacher. It made no difference who was in the right, because the teacher, minister, or any other adult or authority figure always won.

We had some degree of modesty. We didn't pull our pants down and take pictures of our vaginas or penises. We didn't have phones with cameras so we could take selfies. Hell, we didn't even have phones.

101

I don't know a drug store, back in the '50s, that you could take film to that would develop such pictures. If there was one, I doubt that I would have wanted to give a picture of my boobs or pussy to some guy a week or ten days later because that is how long it took to get the pictures back. Some of my relationships barely lasted a week.

I hate what social media has done to today's generation. But, you know what? Now, just like then, it's all about choices.

<u>Bullying</u>

A little girl of six cries herself to sleep,
At this young age, school shouldn't be so hard.
The kids made fun of her, said she was fat,
They teased her and called her a stupid retard.

This sweet girl of ten wipes away the tears,
She looks down at the bruises on her little thin arm.
This time it was three girls who ganged up on her.
Why me, she wonders. I mean them no harm.

Now, fifteen years old, alone and lost in her pain,
She has no one to talk to, her parents don't care.
Her brother is as bad as the rest of his friends,
Teasing her, touching her, and pulling her hair.

The razor is sharp and her thigh is exposed,
She's been cutting now for a couple of years.
This makes her feel good, this brings her relief,
God only knows, it's so much better than tears.

The basement is cold but it's not dark anymore,
Lots of people are crying and wondering why.
They've cut this girl down; now she lies on the floor,
And, none of them know why she decided to die.

slp

Chow Time

In the olden days, like the '50s, mothers cleaned, cooked, baked, washed clothes, and did the ironing. My mother canned a lot in the fall and the shelves in a cold cellar room were usually full by Thanksgiving. After my dad married Florence, he taught her how to can fruits and vegetables. She did a pretty good job but my mother's dill pickles were always the best.

My father always got a deer during hunting season and some of the meat would be used to make mincemeat for mincemeat pie. I hated it, but at least it was one of the few things I wasn't forced to eat.

The butcher shop that cut up his deer also rented freezer space where he could store the meat. After dad bought a big chest freezer for the house, a lot of items that were previously canned were now frozen. It was less work and he no longer had to pay for a freezer in town to store his venison, ducks, and geese.

One year dad decided to cut up his deer and save the cost of having it butchered. It was the end of November and freezing cold out. He had hung the frozen, gutted deer in the garage and told me I had to help him. I was probably sixteen at the time. He made me steady that deer while he skinned it and cut it up. It was probably the worst thing he asked me to do. I still remember how cold my hands were holding that damn deer, even with gloves on.

I was raised on venison. Dad would have sausage made, which we enjoyed. I didn't mind the hamburger but hated the roasts which always tasted a little tallowy. Sometimes, on a Sunday morning, we would have pancakes with little venison steaks. That was considered a real treat. I never enjoyed the ducks and geese that dad shot. I don't recall that he ever went pheasant hunting, but Ray did. I got pretty good at fixing them. Today, you couldn't pay me to eat any of them.

We never went out to eat in a restaurant in town as a family. The only time I ate in a restaurant with dad was when we were traveling.

Picture – Earl's Café - 1956

However, I ate in town a lot after bowling or after a school dance. Earl's Café made the best hamburgers I ever ate. They were greasy and I should have died from clogged arteries years ago. I think they might have cost fifteen cents or a quarter at the time. My friends and I would have a burger and a Coke and listen to the jukebox.

Eating fast food at home for a meal was unheard of. We had a Dairy Queen in town. It was next to Kurth's Brewery. We would walk there on a warm summer night and order a cone or a sundae. Or, we might walk to the other end of town to the A & W for a root beer or a root beer float. They closed during the winter months.

That was it as far as fast-food places go in town back then. There were no McDonald's or Burger Kings and certainly no pizza places. I didn't even try a pizza until I was out of school and working in Madison.

We ate healthy foods with no preservatives. TV dinners weren't being made yet and we ate the meals our mothers made sitting down at a table as a family. The best meals I remember were when dad was on the road and it was only us kids and Florence. Those were fun times.

Vacations

When we were young, we rarely went on a real vacation. What dad called a vacation was a business trip with us being dragged along.

However, after he was married to Florence and Kurt and Virginia had flown the coup, he started to travel just for pleasure. His pleasure. He would take fishing trips when I was a freshman and sophomore in high school. We mostly just sat and watched him fish or tried to entertain ourselves sitting in the car in some God-forgotten place. I don't think some of those places we wound up in were even on the map.

He would stop at one or two lumber companies during these trips, which gave him some tax write-offs.

He loved to drive up to Sault Ste. Marie and watch the boats go through the Soo Locks. It wasn't unusual for us to sit for two to four hours waiting for him to get his fill of Soo seeing and get back on the road.

When I was a junior in high school, we drove up to Batchawana Bay which is in Northeastern Ontario, Canada. Dad rented a cabin and fished his days away while Carol, George, and I played on the beach and wished we were home.

At one point, seeing how bored we were, dad paid the fee, and Carol and I went horseback riding. I didn't really enjoy it and I was sore for a few days after straddling that saddle.

In 1956, dad started going to Florida for vacations. We only stayed a week. In 1957, we took a side trip on our way home and went to New Orleans for Mardi Gras. I had contracted a horrible cold and coughed my lungs out for days. I saw a doctor after we got home and was told I had pleurisy.

Dad went to Florida every year after that. After Carol and George graduated from high school, his vacations became longer and longer. After he retired, he spent a couple of months a year there.

Picture – Susan riding a horse – Batchawana Bay, Canada

As a kid, I wasn't crazy about sitting in a car for hours at a time. As an adult, I appreciate the fact that I saw a lot of the country in its raw form. Today there are highways where there were one-lane dirt roads. Towns where there was only a gas station and a diner.

I guess I kind of have to thank him, even if it's a little late. I got an education that no school could teach.no school could teach.

Let's Party

The legal drinking age in 1956 for drinking beer and wine in Wisconsin was eighteen. I was seventeen and the basketball team had planned a Friday night final game of the season party. It started out being a 'team-only party' at the home of a player whose parents were going to be out of town for the weekend. Word got around and soon about sixty kids showed up, mostly seniors and a few juniors. Everyone chipped in fifty cents for beer and there was plenty to go around. I arrived with my date, did not drink, (which was unusual for me), someone yelled the police are coming about ten minutes after the party started, and we tore out of there.

At school, the following Monday morning, a list of names was read over the loudspeaker. Every student that had been to that party, except for two, was on that list. We were told we had five minutes to report to a classroom where we were then kept waiting for fifteen minutes. We expected to see the principal, so when Superintendent Moser walked in, we knew trouble was brewing. The main man was there.

He informed us that we needed a note from our parents saying they knew about the party and that alcohol had been served. We had until Friday to turn it in – or else.

I sweated it all week and finally, on Thursday night I told my dad that I needed a note which was to say he knew about the party, that I had been there, and that drinking had taken place. He asked me if I drank anything and I, in all honesty, said no. He said, "Type up what you need and I'll sign it," and that was it. He laughed and said he had known about this all week and figured I'd suffered enough.

I would love to know what some of those parents wrote in their notes to the superintendent. I know Pat's dad said that he wished he'd been invited.

I'd like to be able to tell you that the two kids who turned us in to the principal had the crap beaten out of them but I'd be lying. A little name-calling and a few threats were made, but no blood was drawn. I guess we were afraid we'd all be called back into the principal's office.

Afraid – fear – scared – frightened – words that describe our childhood.

Kids my age grew up being afraid - afraid of our parents, our teachers, our ministers and priests, our police, and anyone else in authority. If we questioned them or disrespected them, we were punished.

When my grandson was about five years old, my son threatened him with a spanking if he didn't behave. His response was, "If you hit me, I'll call the police".

The Best Days of My Life

I loved every minute of high school. If I could go back in time, I would be going through the doors of that high school as a brand-new freshman. However, only that particular school with all the same people.

The old main building was three stories. They put an addition on years later that housed the new gym and the basement where the lockers and showers were. We had P.E. classes every day and it was co-ed on Fridays. There weren't many fat kids back then.

The school had two gyms. The older, smaller gym was used for the hot lunch program and dances. There was always a dance after basketball or football games. A huge room on the top floor was used for assembly and free time. We always had one free period and this was mostly used to do school work or sleep.

School started at 8:10 and got out at 4:10 with an hour for lunch. I walked to school in the morning, walked home for lunch, stopped off at the drug store for a Coke, walked back to school, and as soon as school was out, I was back at the drug store. We hung out there a lot. The Corner Drug Store had a counter and three booths in the back. We always got a booth. Cherry cokes and a bag of potato chips were the usual order.

The first few years I was pretty active in school. I was in the glee club, chorus, and intermural activities, all of which took place after school. When I was a junior, I got a job working at the only bakery in town a couple of days a week after school and on Saturdays.

When there weren't any games being played on a Friday night, we hung out in the library basement. There were a couple of good-sized rooms and it housed a jukebox, a ping-pong table, and a small dance floor. There were usually a couple of dozen kids there on any given Friday night, mostly juniors and seniors.

By the time I was a junior, I was out almost every night with my good friend, Karen. Some people thought having five kids in a family was a lot. Karen had eleven brothers and sisters and another family in town had thirteen children.

When I went out during the week, I would say I was going to the library to study. I always stopped at the library (no lies) and then headed to the bowling alley. I started drinking beer there with no problems. Then, when I turned eighteen, I got my Wisconsin I.D. and proudly showed it off at the bar. The owner wasn't too happy with me, but he still took my money and served me. What the hell? It was Columbus. Who really cared?

School came easy to me and I rarely had to study. I got A's in most classes, but it wasn't unusual for a teacher to write an 'unsatisfactory' comment. It seems I was a disturbing influence in class and I could have done better.

I learned a lot during those four years, like how to French kiss a boy and how cool it was to drink and smoke. I never really thought about the future. I knew I'd graduate, leave home, get a job, and go from there.

Then came graduation and suddenly I was faced with reality. I was only a little teenage girl, I was on my own, and I was scared to death.

About That Old Woman

There was an old woman who lived in a shoe,
What a totally weird and strange thing to do.
Was it a shoe of a giant who was over 40 feet tall,
Or, was this old woman just really quite small?

Had this shoe been worn? Did it stink or smell?
Or, were there so many smells, you just couldn't tell?
How many kids before you don't know what to do?
And tell me, how many would actually fit in a shoe?

She fed them broth at a table that held twenty-four,
And even then, some had to sit on the floor.
A whipping they all got, I'd like to know why;
What good does it do to make little kids cry?

They cried and cried and she sent them to bed;
Then, she had some broth and ate all the bread.
To the cupboard she went and poured a stiff drink;
Not the first of the day, I'm beginning to think.

Her story is sad, but we don't know the whole tale;
Perhaps her husband's in jail and she can't
make the bail.
There could be a good reason she's so
mean and so blue;
So don't judge her if you've never lived in a shoe.

<u>It Was the Fifties</u>

There has never been a time like it and there never will be again.

Rock and Roll – Elvis – Fats Domino – The Everly Brother – Sock Dances – Stay at Home Moms – Poodle Skirts and Saddle Shoes – Riding in Cars with Boys – Breaking Curfew – and a million other wonderful things.

'American Graffiti' – You've seen the movie. You know it's true. Even in a little town like Columbus, the streets were cruised. Well, maybe only one or two cars and not every weekend, and a lot of time they were cars with boys from other towns, but it did happen.

My friends and I walked everywhere. Distance made no difference. We walked to high school, we walked to the park, and we walked the streets. Little boy-crazy girls looking for girl-crazy boys. Sometimes we would get picked up and ride around with strange boys. Nothing ever happened. We would drive up and down the streets and talk and act like we'd see each other again but we never did. Then, we'd get dropped off and home we'd go. What the hell were we thinking? No fear. Never scared. We could have been raped or murdered. It was the fifties and it was a much safer time. But still....

I'd had little girl crushes before I started high school. The truth is, I was scared to even talk to boys. I was in the sixth grade when I saw Phil walking down the street on Valentine's Day carrying a box of candy, I hid in my own house. Virginia answered the door and he gave the candy to her to give to me. The next day I thanked him and ran in the other direction.

In seventh grade, I got my first huge crush on a boy. It was the first day of school. Ray was in eighth grade and preparing for confirmation so he had to go to parochial school. The minute I saw him, I wanted him. And he couldn't stand me.

My sister, Virginia, introduced me to Bob when I was in the eighth grade. He was a junior in high school and we had absolutely nothing in common to talk about, so all we ever did was neck. He was the first boy to touch my boobies, which weren't even fully developed. I was so naïve that I didn't even realize that he did it on purpose. So, I guess he was the first guy to get to second base.

When I was a freshman, I dated Norman for a while. He was nineteen at the time. My father finally put a stop to that relationship and Norman joined the Marines and left town.

I'm still confused as to why my dad allowed me to date older guys when I was so young. At least nothing more than a little boob touch ever happened, but they were way too old for me.

I never really went out on a 'date' with Ray while I was in school, but there were times that we would be together with a group of kids. We kissed a few times and then I wouldn't see him for months. He finally joined the army and was gone.

I guess my first real love was Pat. He was the best guy I ever went with and the boy I probably should have married. Pat and I were dating when Ray came home on leave. Even though I was going 'steady' with Pat, I went out on a date with Ray. Pat was waiting for me when Ray dropped me off and that was that. I broke his heart. I loved Pat but I was still crazy for that no-good bad boy, Ray.

Picture - Phonograph for 78s and 45s. Susan

I married Ray a year after I graduated from high school. I have made a lot of mistakes in my life, but this is at the top of the list.

A little piece of me has always loved Pat and always will. I think it's true that you always love your first.

And, as far as Ray. . . Well, as the saying goes - be careful what you wish for.

<u>Blueberry Hill</u>

We're parked in my, car after the prom, where
We had danced to the JAILHOUSE ROCK.
I'm in <u>A WHITE SPORTS COAT AND</u>
<u>A PINK CARNATION,</u>
And <u>LITTLE SUZIE'S</u> in her pretty blue frock

My best bud's in the back seat with his
<u>LITTLE DARLIN'.</u>
I hope he behaves and doesn't make her <u>CRY.</u>
She says <u>THERE'S LIPSTICK ON YOUR COLLAR;</u>
<u>AIN'T THAT A SHAME,</u> is his stupid reply.

I look in my girl's eyes, feeling her love when
She says <u>I WAS BORN TO BE WITH YOU.</u>
But, <u>WILL YOU STILL LOVE ME TOMORROW,</u> I ask
and hear her say
Only if you stay away from <u>RUNAROUND SUE.</u>

Each night there are <u>TEARS ON MY PILLOW,</u>
Thinking of that horrible time.
How do I know <u>YOUR CHEATIN' HEART</u> is
gone for good?
<u>TRUST IN ME,</u> I say softly, 'cause <u>I WALK THE LINE.</u>

I'm going to <u>TAKE GOOD CARE OF MY BABY,</u>
I whisper,
And, the night becomes suddenly still as
She wraps her body around me and then----
I found my thrill on <u>BLUEBERRY HILL.</u>

<u>Breaking Bad</u>

My mother swore she carried me for ten months. It's possible that I ventured down that direction a few times but, when I heard all that fighting going on, I crawled right back up into her womb. I eventually did arrive at the hefty weight of five pounds and I was born with Rickets. Rickets is usually caused by a vitamin D deficiency or a lack of calcium and the result can be weak and/or deformed bones. People with this disease usually live in third-world countries, so I guess mother didn't get enough calcium from her beer or those taverns were just too dark to let the sun in. Or, perhaps living in the backwoods of Idaho, where dad ran a logging camp in 1939 was like living in a third-world country.

I refused my mother's milk from the beginning and nothing the doctor tried seemed to stay down. Eventually, a nursing mother goat who had plenty of milk gave me the nourishment I needed to survive and I lived. I lucked out and didn't get any deformed bones so I looked normal, but my bones have always been brittle. Although the doctor told my parents I would never be healthy, I actually grew up the healthiest one in the family. Mentally and physically. I know this is hard to believe but, seriously, I've been told on many occasions by many people that I am the sanest one in the family.

I waited until 1956 to break my first bone. It happened during gym class when, while playing basketball, I went one way, my foot went the other, and snap. I broke a bone in my foot. I spent the next six weeks in a cast and on crutches. Even though it was winter, it didn't slow me down and I 'step and a halved it' all over town. During school, I was usually picked up by some strong boy or a teacher like Mr. Wray and carried up the steps.

"The next time you decide to hit your husband, use a brick." was the advice the doctor gave me after I broke one bone and cracked three more in my right hand. Ray and I were goofing around and I slugged him. I was aiming for his arm but he moved and I punched him in his jaw. My bad.

I had a few more broken bones after this, a gift of husband number three. I didn't stay around for more. There is no excuse for a man to hit a woman. There's no excuse for a woman to hit a man, either. And, there's absolutely, positively no excuse to stay in a violent marriage.

SOME AFTERTHOUGHTS AND STUFF

Picture – Bruce, Perry, Arthur, Nick, Jon, Jon – 1988 – 89

And 2 Makes 5

When Bruce was a little over a year old, I decided it was time to give him a playmate. I got pregnant but lost that baby. A few months after the miscarriage, I got pregnant with Jon.

Ray and I were living in Fox Lake, Wisconsin when Jon was born on January 14, 1961. Jon was the first baby born in that town that year. The newspaper interviewed me and my picture was in the paper holding my brand-new baby.

Most of the stores in town had some type of gift they gave for that honor. I can't remember what they were now, except for the bank which opened a savings account for him for $5.00. It's still there.

Obviously, we lived in a small town.

We were living in Federal Way, Washington when Perry was born. Jon was only one year and two weeks old. Bruce had recently turned three. Three months after Perry came along, I miscarried again. This time I lost twins. imagine – I would have had five kids under the age of four.

I do believe God doesn't give you more than you can handle, especially as a few years later I was raising my boys as a single mother

.

Don't Piss God Off!

Even though I hated going to the Lutheran School, I have to admit that I learned a lot about religion. The Bible is really a good book. I believe the bible is mostly a true book, but let's not forget that men wrote it. We know that most men don't listen when you're talking to them. (ask any woman) Therefore, I have to wonder if they didn't get some of the stories in the bible a little mixed up.

I do believe that God created the earth and man and that he did send his son, Jesus, to save us. The problem may be that there were too many authors, like Moses and David, and some of the disciples. It was written over so many years that things might have become confused. In addition, a lot of wine was drunk in those days, which may have caused some of these stories to be more than a little embellished.

If all the stories have been written down exactly as they happened, then God either has a mean streak or a really sick sense of humor. Let's take Job, for instance.

God was tough on Job. God's old angel friend, the Devil, who had been cast into hell, still had a relationship (a strange one indeed) with God. They saw each other occasionally and usually argued about the way of the world and probably global warming. (I hear that conversation has been going on for a long time.)

The Devil still wanted to control the world even though God had already kicked his ass in a previous power struggle. Anyway, one day the Devil and God were having this conversation and the Devil said he didn't think there was one good, faithful man left on earth that couldn't be corrupted or wouldn't turn away from God.

"Looks like you're losing them by the thousands and it looks like sin wins," the Devil told God.

However, God challenged him and God said he still had plenty of faithful followers who would never lose their faith no matter how bad things got.

"Prove it, God," said the Devil.

So, God pulled up a couple of chairs, poured a couple of drinks from a vintage bottle of scotch, lit up a really good Cuban cigar, put up his feet, and said, "Let's see who is right and who is wrong."

Of course, we all know how that went. Job suffered beyond belief, and lost everything - even his kids - but he kept his faith. In fact, when this bet ended, he got everything back, plus more good stuff from God. The devil lost and God won. But, seriously, simply to win a bet? That's really kind of mean, don't you think?

Did God have to flood the earth? It seems there would have been an easier way to shape up all the sinners. Noah was the only one who listened, and did what he was told, and what was his reward? Ok, he and his family were saved, but can you even imagine the stink on that ark? Two of every animal, bird, and insect – peeing and pooping for forty days. Can anyone really shovel that much shit? It must have been a full-time job for him and his family trying to keep up with the mess.

God must have been totally pissed about something or bored the day he decided that Jewish men should be circumcised. Abraham was 99 years old when he had his foreskin cut off. It didn't make any difference if you were Jewish or what age you were, you had to stand in line and wait your turn. Even if you were a slave and owned by a Jew, off it came. I imagine there was a lot of wailing and screaming that day when one pecker after another was subjected to mutilation by some guy who had never done this before and had no idea what he was doing. Can you even imagine being the first in line for that snip job?

That whining, bitching Jonah must have been pretty stupid when God told him to go one way and he went the other. "I'm not going to Nineveh," he whined. "They'll fricking kill me." So, he hopped on the first boat and headed in the opposite direction. He bitched about the food on the fishing boat and that his lodgings weren't good enough. He complained about the weather and the storm. Then, when the sailors picked him up and threw him overboard, he really threw a hissy fit.

I'll save him, God thought. I'm not done with him yet but he is going to pay for not obeying me and for all his bitching, which is driving me nuts.

For three days, Jonah was in the guts of a whale. God could have as easily grabbed him out of that whale and thrown him ashore to save his life. I guess, though, that it was a lot more fun to stick him in a stinky, foul-smelling belly of a beast for three days.

What about scaring little kids? Testing your faith is one thing, but do you have to scare the crap out of a kid doing it?

"Abraham, go get Isaac, tie him up, blindfold him, and lay him on a rock. Then, get that knife that you use on the sacrificial lambs when you cut their throats and stab him. And - after you're done doing that - how about torching him?"

Hey, are we having fun yet?

124

So, is he a mean God or a prankster? He tells us that he is a vengeful God. I think he is also a very loving but sad and disappointed God who, like any parent, continues to hope his rotten kids will learn their lessons and turn out okay.

Just a last word here. I meant no disrespect to God when I wrote this chapter. They're things that I sometimes think about. I mean, like, it's all so confusing, isn't it?

Willie

Honeysuckle Rose, *Wag The Dog*, and on and on the movie list goes. I think I like Honeysuckle Rose the best because of the music.

I don't remember exactly when I fell in love with Willie, but it's a love that has lasted forever.

I've been to many of his concerts and never tire of his music, be it Country, Modern, or the Blues.

I do believe I have almost all of his albums, except for the one that recently came out.

Picture – Willie and Me – Branson

Willie played in Branson for a while, if you recall. He managed to make enough to pay off the IRS and get the hell out of Dodge.

I went to his concert there, too. I probably would have gone to every concert he had while I was there, but the friend I was with hated country music. She bad.

Books

 My mother was considered tall at five feet ten and a half inches. She was only an inch shorter than my father.

I was the shortest one in the family, topping out at five feet four and a half inches. Being six inches shorter than my mother, I always had to look up at her. The older she got the shorter she became and the last time I saw her she was shorter than me. I have no idea how short she was when she died but, at the rate she was going, she was probably only a couple of feet tall.

Even though her boobs weren't huge, when my dad was in a teasing mood, he sometimes called her 'big tit Liz'. I have no idea where the nickname came from or who Liz was, but that was the only pet name I ever heard him call her.

Picture – a chamber pot

I thought that my mother was beautiful. Her skin was flawless and I don't believe she ever had a blemish. She was a clothes horse and loved to wear hats. I think she could have put a chamber pot on her head and looked good in it. She sewed beautifully and made most of her clothes.

My mother never worked outside of the house while married to my dad. Her talents were unlimited and she excelled at anything that she attempted. She was extremely intelligent and most of her jobs, after she left my father, were in accounting. She opened a number of different businesses, then got bored with them or decided to leave town, and walked away leaving someone else to clean up her messes.

My mother was one of the most talented persons I have ever known. She played the piano and the organ and she had a beautiful singing voice.

She was a fantastic cook and baker. She was hired by numerous people to make cakes for parties and weddings. She made my son's wedding cake and it was beautiful and delicious.

She sewed like a tailor. At one time she opened her own store in Beaver Dam, Wisconsin, and called it Ruth's Sew and Sew Shop. Before she left us, she made most of our clothes. When Virginia got married, she made her wedding dress and the two bridesmaid dresses.

Whatever project she took on, she did it well.

And – she loved to read. I never saw her without a book. I sometimes wonder if reading all those books gave her the wanderlust that made her leave her family and go and go and go. I cannot begin to count the times that she moved after she left us, but it had to be well over one hundred. She moved to Alaska, Texas, back to Montana, Washington, Illinois, Wisconsin, and Oregon. What have I missed? She would move into an apartment, get a job, stay for a while, and, then, she was gone. Off to a new adventure, but eventually moving to be close to where Virginia was living.

Even when she stayed in one town, she would move a couple of times, always needing something newer or better.

I turned out fairly talented, so I guess I got some of the good stuff from her. But, the one thing that I truly appreciate is that I inherited her love of books. From the time I can remember, I've read. Even when I was in high school, I read three or four books a week.

I'm truly grateful for that. Thanks, Mom.

Man – What Was God Thinking?

God created a wonderful, majestic world. He placed trees in forests and fields, along the riverbanks, and high in the mountains. He placed glaciers to the north and south of our earth and clear, warm tropic waters in the middle. He did everything right and it was beautiful to behold.

He added the animals, the birds, and the insects that inhabited his wondrous work and they lived in peace and harmony.

Then, for some reason, he decided that our earth needed a caretaker to watch over this glorious globe and he made man. Now we all understand that God probably has lots of planets and worlds that he created and I'm sure they are all beautiful in different ways. While ours is green with blue oceans and white with snow, some are probably red and rosy and smell rotten. For all we know there could be a whole bunch of rainbow-colored planets. Perhaps, he was tired of looking after all of them and decided to make strange-looking upright walking beings to do it for him. Therefore - man. And, then - woman (let's not even go there).

He did our earth no favor by putting man, who only uses about 5% of his brain, in the picture. Slowly man is destroying his work. Less slowly, I think God is getting angrier and angrier.

Now here is where I get confused. If he hadn't created man, there would have been no need for Jesus. Now, Jesus came to save us from the sins of man, but these sins were occurrences that God decided were sins. If he hadn't created temptations, sins, and all that shit, the world would have stayed a wonderful, peaceful world. Wouldn't it have been better to leave the world to animals, birds, and insects? And, no talking snakes, please. He's 'all-seeing' so he had to have seen this coming. Tell me this isn't confusing.

Getting past the fact that he did make man, then the biggest flaw I see here is the design of man itself. Two legs are good. One head is good. Two eyes not so great, but three eyes are perfect. There should be at least one eye in the back of the head, so we can see where we are going and where we have been. Mothers especially need that third eye. No one could ever sneak up on us and there would be fewer sneak attacks.

Two ears look good and function badly. It would have been better to have had earflaps that we can open and close, so we can have subjective hearing. This is something that I am sure men would pay thousands of dollars to have. Just think. No more blah, blah, blah to listen to.

All noses should be beautiful, regardless of anything. They should look good and be placed exactly right.

Women's boobs should be sized according to the woman's body. Not too big or too small and they should be completely done growing by the age of sixteen. They should never change no matter what the circumstance. Breastfeeding, they stay the same. Old age, they still look like they did when they were sixteen. No enhancements ever allowed. You are what you are and you get what you get.

Sex organs. What was he thinking? They should be totally separate from any bodily bathroom discharge areas. Of course, I doubt he even imagined that 'going down' would become so popular. Or, did he? This could be God playing one more huge, stinky joke on us.

Most important, however, is the design of arms and hands. We should have three of each. Just think if you could hold the piece of wood with one hand, hold the nail with the second hand, and hammer with the third.

Also, I've recently noticed that if you walk with a cane, it would help immensely if you could be doing or carrying things with two hands while holding a cane with the third.

Again – no disrespect intended.

Picture - Columbus House built 1900

<u>As Time Goes By</u>

So, my dear sons, you know most of the rest of the story. I was married to your dad for nine years. You have numerous brothers and sisters throughout the country and perhaps the world. After all, he was stationed in Germany when he was in the Army. I'm sure he donated a lot of sperm while he was there.

One time we tried to count your half-siblings that we knew about for sure and I believe it was around fifty. Just kidding, but it might be for all we know. He honestly couldn't keep it in his pants.

<u>Picture – Jon, Bruce, Jon, Nick, Perry</u>

I raised you the best I could and I'm proud of how you all turned out. I watched you grow into wonderful hard-working men. Best of all, I love that you inherited my sense of humor and enjoy a good laugh. Never stop seeing the humor in what comes your way and never be afraid to shed a tear. Give a person a hug when they need it and welcome one back with open arms.

Always tell your kids you love them. It's something they can't hear enough.

Thanks for the grandsons. They are the best and I love it when I get a chance to visit with them. You've done a good job, too. I'm still waiting for a great, so get on their butts, will you?

Maybe someday I'll write you a book about my years between graduating from high school and the present. Like when we lived in Washington and I almost shot your dad. Ah, regrets. I've had a few.

So much to tell and yet so much to keep secret.

Love you, boys.

Mom

About the Author

I was born in Idaho in 1939. My father's job demanded that we frequently move and, by the age of ten, I had lived in Idaho, Montana, Colorado, Michigan, and Wisconsin.

I am the proud mother of three wonderful sons and two fantastic grandsons. I have no plans to acquire another husband, as they are too much work.

For most of my life, I worked as an accountant. Two years before I retired, I did a complete switch in careers and managed two Curves fitness facilities in Illinois. I retired in 2002 and moved to Branson, MO. In 2012, I moved to Indiana to be closer to my family and have resided in Highland since then.

I enjoy a good laugh and figure it's my sense of humor that keeps me going when times are tough. Reading has always been one of my passions and I still read a couple of books a week.

In 2014, I wrote my first book, *Blueberries and Bears and My Brother's Shoes*, a book about growing up in the forties and fifties. After I self-published it and gave it to friends and family to read, they encouraged me to get serious about my writing.

I never thought that, at the age of 76, I would become an author. I set a goal for myself to write at least ten books before I die. I've made the ten-plus and I'm pretty sure I have a lot more novels kicking around in this head of mine.

I certainly am enjoying my retirement knowing, when I get up each morning, I have something to look forward to. You can find out more about me and my books at my website. Please visit me there, sign up to be on my readers' list, and feel free to send me your comments.

www.susanlpare.com

REVIEWS FROM ACTUAL READERS
Of SUSAN'S BOOKS

THE HOUSE ON LUDINGTON STREET
Review by Nick B

Susan Pare once again writes something that you will not be able to put down as a reader. Her stories have always been captivating but this novel is a new approach for her. She took what her old novels did so well and added new elements to The House on Ludington Street. For those television viewers out there this novel is a blend of American Horror Story and Haunting of Hill House. Throw in some dark humor and binge-read away. Her twists and turns continue to impress and the development of characters makes you care about what you are reading. Another terrific piece of writing by Ms. Pare!

DON'T SMOTHER YOUR MOTHER (A Sheriff "Cowboy" Berkson Mystery Novel – Book One)
Review by John H

Well, Susan has done it again. Kept my rapt attention from beginning to end. This isn't my first rodeo with Susan. I love her writing, style, and suspense. One thing everyone will probably notice: As you read you start to think of people you used to know who are just like the characters in the book. Usually poignant, sometimes funny, sometimes people you'd just like to go back to forgetting. LOVED THIS BOOK. KEEP IT UP, SUSAN !!

CROSSING SYDNEY
Review by Laurie L

No matter how sophisticated a reader you are, Crossing Sydney is going to surprise you. A unique plot that keeps you riveted until the very end where you'll find yourself going back to read the last few pages just in case you missed something. You didn't - you were delightfully and masterfully tricked.

THE MAYOR'S SON
Review by Kevin Q

A simple town, a simple time ... and two ghastly crimes. Having grown up in small-town America, I appreciated the undercurrents throughout the story. Cops, parents, friends, and neighbors thinking they know everything there is to know about the goings-on around town ... only to find out otherwise. I found Susan's work to be an entertaining read that flowed well, kept me engaged, and provided a sufficient amount of suspense all the way to the surprise ending. Well done ...

WILLERTON WOODS
Review by Jon B

Pare' does it again. Her latest mystery novel is definitely a page-turner and you won't want to put it down until you know for sure who is who and what is what and who's done what. I love the twists and turns of the story and how the writer brings it all together at the end. I can't wait for her next novel. This is a good read and just the right number of pages for me. I give it five stars and highly recommend it.

THE HOUSE ON LUDINGTON STREET
Review by Julie M

Susan Pare, the author, used to live in my house years ago and this is the House on Ludington Street! I've lived in the city for about 9 years and it was fun to read about some familiar places. I teach reading at a nearby community college.

The class is at college-level, but my students aren't quite there and reading is the best strategy for improving reading. Every semester, I have a rather unique semester-long project where the students get to choose a book, fact or fiction, by a Wisconsin author that they would like to read. Susan Pare's books would work well for some of my students. I am adding her books to our collection because they are a manageable length and would appeal to my students.

WHAT'S BEHIND THE SCREEN DOOR
Review by Bruce B

Over the past few years, I have enjoyed reading Susan Pare's books and have come to look forward to her next release. Behind the Screen Door once again did not disappoint keeping me engaged the entire read. What a refreshing and intriguing author. If you have read any of Susan's books you learn to absolutely "EXPECT THE UNEXPECTED."

FLOATING FACE DOWN, A Sheriff "Cowboy" Berkson Mystery Novel
Review by Michael J

This is the final book of a 3 book series. All 3 stories are written in a simple style that most small town folks can relate to. The stories had a lot of different plot changes that involved mostly around one family and always seemed to keep one guessing as to what would happen next. For me, it was hard to put the books down once I started to read them, as they really kept my interest up, and I was also able to read through each one rather quickly. I also liked the fact that at the end, one has the ability to use one's own imagination as to what else may have happened in the future if the storyline was then continued. Just simply fun, enjoyable reading in my opinion

.